the CELTIC BOOK of the DEAD

the CELTIC

BOOK

of the
DEAD

A GUIDE FOR YOUR VOYAGE
TO THE CELTIC OTHERWORLD

Caitlín Matthews

CARDS ILLUSTRATED BY
DANUTA MAYER

A THOMAS · DUNNE
BOOK

ST. MARTIN'S
P R E S S

Library of Congress Cataloging-in-Publication Data

Matthews, Caitlín
    The Celtic Book of the Dead / Caitlín Matthews.
        p.   cm.
    "A Thomas Dunne Book"
    ISBN 0-312-07241-4
    1. Divination.   2. Ritual.   1. Title.
    BF1751.M37   1992
    133.3'089'916—DC20   91-29086
                                              CIP

First U.S. Edition: May 1992

10 9 8 7 6 5 4 3 2 1

AN EDDISON · SADD EDITION
Edited, designed and produced by
Eddison Sadd Editions Limited
St Chad's Court
146B King's Cross Road
London WC1X 9DH

Phototypeset in Berkeley Oldstyle and Delphin by
Wyvern Typesetting, Bristol, England
Origination by Columbia Offset, Singapore
Produced in Hong Kong by Mandarin Offset
Printed and bound in Hong Kong

For Therese Schroeder-Sheker
who has piloted many souls
across these waters
by means of music.

Acknowledgements

Thanks to Manannan mac Lír, Posula, Melusine, Diarmuid and the totems. To all my students who have taken the otherworldly voyage with me, especially those who allowed me to use their readings in Chapter Five. To John and Emrys Matthews, for bailing me out and drying me off after stormy *immrama*. To Paul Brady, surfer supreme, and Felicity Aldridge, scryer of waters, for sharing knowledge of Tír fa Thon, the Celtic Land Under Wave. A special thank-you to Mary McLaughlin whose help and insight brought my voice back across the waters. I warmly acknowledge the artistic work of Danuta Mayer who took the *immram* and saw the wonders for herself and the scholarship of H.P.A. Oskamp, from whose edition of the *Voyage of Maelduin* I made my translation. To Robin Willliamson, many thanks for permission to quote his inspirational song *The Circle is Unbroken*. The peace of the *sidhe* and a smooth *immram* upon all who have helped me prepare this project.

The illustration on page 17 is by Anton Sorg, from *Voyage of St Brendan*, Augsburg, 1476.

EDDISON · SADD EDITIONS

Editor	Michele Doyle
Designer	Sarah Howerd
Art Director	Elaine Partington
Proofreader	Jennifer Strachan
Lettering Artist	Jim Gibson
Production	Hazel Kirkman and Charles James

worlds within. Since the Western world abandoned its inner cosmology, the geography of the spiritual realms is a mystery and the journey beyond life fraught with terror. This is made no easier by the fact that we are often totally ignorant of the alternative realities that can empower us. Although most of Western humanity has ceased to be convinced by orthodox spiritualities, finding heaven and hell equally redundant, it has nevertheless begun a series of quests for meaning. One of these quests looks back to the time before Christianity, to the old spiritual traditions of the earth that preserve a healthy sense of alternative reality. Such traditions as the Native American, the Sami (Lapp) and Shinto have a concept of the integration of life and death with nature. This concept was also once part of our own north-west European tradition.

Within Celtic tradition, lying dormant but dynamically potent, is the *Celtic Book of the Dead*. The Celts did not have books but a vibrant oral tradition preserved by poets, story-tellers and druids who regulated and enriched society by the recitation of traditional lore in the form of stories. One collection of these spiritual stories was called *immrama*, meaning 'mystical voyages'. At least four complete sets of these stories remain. The most famous *immram* is the *Voyage of St Brendan* which describes that Irish saint's peregrinations by means of a skin boat to the Isles of the West. Brendan's voyage has been considered by many as a charming hagiological tale with little warrant in reality. But some modern travellers, like Tim Severin, the famous reconstructor of historical voyages, believe that Brendan's voyage has its roots in fact. Severin actually re-enacted Brendan's voyage from Ireland, around Britain and across the Atlantic, landing in Newfoundland: the first such voyage by curragh (skin boat) since the Dark Ages.

The *Voyage of St Brendan* enjoyed great popularity in Europe, possibly stimulating the Renaissance urge to discover new lands by means of voyages of exploration. It is significant that interest in the spiritual voyage to the Otherworld gradually became replaced by the actual voyage to find the New World. The erosion of mystical traditions that has marked the gradual colonization by Europe of the known world is a legacy with which the Old World has to find ways of coming to terms.

Brendan's Christian adventures are certainly based upon earlier, pre-

Christian *immrama*, which follow a similar itinerary to that of Brendan. Heroes like Bran mac Febal and Maelduin sail out to the West and find a series of islands, each representing a state in the Celtic Otherworld.

The Celtic Otherworld was believed to have a reality contiguous to and sometimes overlapping ordinary reality. The Celts had no heaven or hell. Their Otherworld, like their philosophy, was non-dual in character. In theory, anyone could reach the Otherworld, which was conceived to be found most easily in the lands to the West. For the Celts, West meant the great Atlantic Ocean and the place of complementary reality.

Throughout the course of European history, myths of lands to the West abound. Most of us are familiar with Avalon, the place of King Arthur's restoration. The drowned lands of Ys and Lyonesse form a prime part of Breton and Cornish folklore. Myths of the land of Atlantis, the mighty civilization that sank beneath the waves, all help sustain the Celtic belief in the Isles of the Blessed to which travellers sail and do not return.

Books of the dead clearly depict states of awareness, specific functions and duties. They show us the guardians and entities who sit at the boundaries between life and death and help resolve and conclude the unfinished business of life, challenging and sorting through neglected responsibilities as life's assessors. Although some books of the dead depict a final judgement – the *Egyptian Book of the Dead*, for example – the Celtic *immram* does not. Instead, each soul contains its own judgement. The Celtic Otherworld is a mirror of this world, so our individual experience of the realm beyond death is influenced by our actions in this life. One of the *immram* islands, the Island of Black and White – where black items turn white and white items turn black – gives us a perception of this. The terrors that travellers meet there are the life lessons from which they have failed to learn or to assimilate. As in both the Egyptian and Tibetan Books of the Dead, the *immrama* stories present some terrifying beings and challenging scenarios. These beings are the threshold guardians of the Celtic tradition; they are not demons or devils, and no more evil than the wrathful deities of Tibet. Their nature is to guard, guide and challenge.

As we have now seen, the function of the *immram* was to teach the craft of dying and to pilot the departing spirit on a sea of perils and wonders. It may also be used, however, by those facing critical decisions or problems, to help them 'cross over'. Using the *immram* of Maelduin, I have prepared *The Celtic Book of the Dead* to act as a guide through the perilous realms of the otherworldly islands, which may be encountered as readily in this life as in the next. Upon each island, new challenges must be met, and strange beings and guardians encountered. Each experience is depicted upon a card, part of a set that forms the journey of the soul to the otherworldly regions. These experiences are fully detailed in this book, which accompanies the forty-two cards. Chapter One explores the Celtic tradition, while in Chapter Two a retelling and the full text of the poem of the *Voyage of Maelduin* is given with commentary and background. Full details of laying and interpreting the cards are given in Chapters Three to Five, while Chapter Six explores further applications of *The Celtic Book of the Dead*, including shamanic journeying and counselling the dying.

The Celtic Book of the Dead is not a morbid exercise of the imagination because, in Celtic tradition, the Otherworld is a place of heightened reality where the great gods dwell; and where the fullness of personal potential is revealed. It is not a place of ghosts or horrors, as in Christian and classical traditions. Instead, we find islands of plenteous salmon, feasting halls and pillars of silver rising from the sea. There are many challenges in the shape of great beasts, formidable giants, islands of unceasing laughter and tears, but each has its lesson to teach.

In an age when many people are striving to change their lives and to align themselves with the principles of ancient yet practical belief-systems, *The Celtic Book of the Dead* offers a way of looking at alternative realities that the Western world has ignored for too long. The *immrama* stories spring from a timeless tradition. I hope that through your study of this book they will become a firm part of Western tradition once more: a life-enhancing celebration of your own voyage through life and beyond.

Caitlín Matthews
Midsummer's Eve 1991

the Celtic World

We will keep faith until the sky falls upon us and crushes us, until the earth opens and swallows us, until the seas arise and overwhelm us.

Celtic oath of the elements

CLAN OF THE ELEMENTS

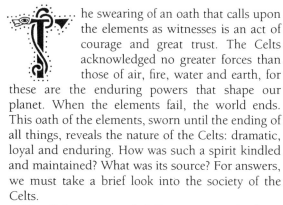

he swearing of an oath that calls upon the elements as witnesses is an act of courage and great trust. The Celts acknowledged no greater forces than those of air, fire, water and earth, for these are the enduring powers that shape our planet. When the elements fail, the world ends. This oath of the elements, sworn until the ending of all things, reveals the nature of the Celts: dramatic, loyal and enduring. How was such a spirit kindled and maintained? What was its source? For answers, we must take a brief look into the society of the Celts.

The Celts were a tribal European people about whose origins scholars are still arguing. Their distinct identity may have had its origins in the Bronze-Age Urnfield culture of northern Europe, dated about 1200–700 BC, so called because it cremated its dead and buried their remains in clay urns. A distinctive Celtic Iron-Age culture is discernible around Hallstat in upper Austria between 700–500 BC, to be followed by a further development around La Tène, in Switzerland, from about 500 BC onwards. These names are used by archae-ologists to determine phases in Celtic culture, but they give us no notion of who the Celts were.

We associate the Celts with the distinctive inter-laced knotwork that typifies their artefacts, and this is a good way of thinking about them. Celtic knot-work is composed of sinuous, intertwined curves that change their form while remaining within the central pattern. This describes the Celts themselves. They were a people bound together by conservative traditions and organized into class-structured tribes. Agriculture underpinned the economy, with the lowest classes of society working the land. Craftspeople received considerable respect. Chief-tains and kings ruled, rewarding their followers with land, while bands of warriors kept the tribal boundaries free of enemies. The law-makers and keepers of traditional lore were the druids, bards and ovates (seers and augurers), whose status was equal to that of the king. Women retained a certain legal independence; we have records of women being warriors, teachers, prophetesses, crafts-women, bards and druids.

In such a fiercely tribal society, notions of honour were paramount. Most of the laws concern loss of honour, insult and recompense to the injured party or his family. As feuds were a common means of settling scores, so fosterage was an important facet of society. Fosterage involved the reception of a young child from one family into a neighbouring family. It was a widespread custom creating bonds of loyalty and obligation that connected families, and was regarded as a sacred duty, like hospitality.

Celtic society recognized individual effort and achievement with high honours: the best warrior received the choicest cut of meat, the most beautiful woman would receive a song in her honour, the most skilful craftsperson would receive a seat in the king's hall. This is still so today: the Celts honour their musicians, poets and tribal customs in special competitive assemblies like the Irish *feis*, the Gaelic *mod*, the Welsh *eisteddfod* and the Highland games in Scotland. This recognition of excellence had its converse side: those who did not uphold the tribal virtues of generosity or courage might expect a satire to be made about them. The satire, in the mouth of a skilled poet, could be a devastating weapon causing considerable loss of face.

The Celts left no written records, since their society was an oral one. We must not take this as evidence of ignorant illiteracy since the Celts, in common with other indigenous cultures, possessed a complex and subtle society based on traditions maintained by skilled memorizers.

How, then, do we know so much about them? The Celts left remarkably beautiful artefacts that speak eloquently about themselves and their concerns. Much of their oral lore, including law tracts, stories, historical chronologies and genealogies, was transcribed by bards turned clerics during the early Celtic Christian era. In a traditional society such as theirs, innovation and improvisation were not encouraged, so we may be sure that many traditions have been passed down to us more or less intact. We also have the evidence of classical writers who came into contact with the Celts and noted down what they observed. Some of these reports show a notable racial bias, for the Celts were regarded by the 'civilized world' as barbarians: this is especially so in the writings of Julius Caesar who had a vested

interest in conquering the Celtic kingdoms. Others, in a more tolerant spirit, provide us with invaluable information: Diodorus Siculus (c. 60–21 BC), Pomponius Mela (first century AD) and Posidonius of Apamea, Syria (c. 135–50 BC) give us both geographical and cultural information.

The classical world encountered the Celts most often in military situations. The Celtic chieftain, Brennos, marched on Greece and sacked Delphi in 279 BC, relieving it of its vast treasury and absconding with it to Gaul, to the horror of all Greeks. Celtic tribes made alliances with both Etruscans and Samnites against the Romans. Celts served as soldiers in Egypt for Ptolemy II. The Roman conquest of Spain and Gaul, both Celtic countries, was followed by the conquest of Britain. But Rome did not conquer Ireland; that task was left to the Normans. The physical and cultural isolation of Ireland ensured that Celtic society continued there in microcosm, sometimes developing its own customs, but mostly adhering to the tribal mores of earlier times. It is in Ireland, therefore, that we find the most enduring evidence.

The Roman invasion of Britain saw a gradual assimilation of Celtic deities and customs into the cosmopolitan, pagan Roman religion. When this was replaced by Christianity, many other Celtic elements were incorporated into its practices. A distinctive Celtic, Christian Church grew up in Gaul, Britain and Ireland, producing such people as St Martin of Tours, St Germanus, St David, St Patrick, St Brighid, St Ninnian and Pelagius, Britain's most famous heretic who disputed with St Augustine of Hippo in the early fifth century.

From the sixth century onwards, Celtic missionaries were sent into Europe where they were busy converting the pagan kingdoms of what are now France, the Rhineland, Switzerland and Austria. Interestingly, the Celtic monks settled in the original Celtic homelands from whence their people had migrated in 500 BC. Celtic Christianity retained many of its pagan features, including druidic methods of tonsure. This involved shaving the head from ear to ear, thus leaving the forehead bare of hair. The Gaulish saint, Hilary of Poitiers (315–367) wrote his *De Trinitate* on the mystery of the Holy Trinity, thereby incorporating for all time the Celtic concept of triplicity into Christianity. Celtic Christianity differed in many ways from the customs of the Roman Church, including the dating of Easter. The Synod of Whitby in 663 was convened to smooth out these irregularities but, in so doing, it robbed the Celtic Church of much of its autonomy. The treasures of Celtic Christianity are slowly beginning to be appreciated once more in our own time.

From the Celtic countries were derived the great stories of King Arthur and the Holy Grail, to be taken to Europe by Celtic story-tellers and further transcribed and adapted by medieval French romancers.

The political picture was less rosy. Conquest and centralized government have been the major burdens of the Celtic countries. Their individual needs, languages and customs have been continually discounted over many hundreds of years, a fact that underlies the tendency of the atavistic Celtic tribal spirit to return as terrorism. Nevertheless, the Celtic spirit has endured, refined and chastened by its historical struggle, producing artists, orators, craftspeople and countless spiritual explorers.

The High Celtic age is no more, but the modern Celts are still very much with us. Their descendants inhabit the western seaboard of Europe in Brittany, Wales, Ireland and Scotland, the last strongholds of Celtic culture. Other migrations due to economic pressures and persecution have led the Celts to spread all over the world, with particular concentrations in parts of the USA, Canada and Australia. Breton, Welsh, and Gaelic are still spoken with enthusiasm as everyday languages in Brittany, Wales, Scotland and Ireland; although faced with the encroaching influence of the media, they are often stubbornly maintained.

The great revival in things Celtic during the twentieth century is very encouraging, for there are many treasures to be discovered, if we only look for them. These riches do not lie only in archaeological artefacts and in existing cultural resources, but in the wealth of the Celtic Otherworld that still informs this ancient tradition.

GUARDIANS OF THE OTHERWORLD

The Celts believed implicitly in the Otherworld, a realm contiguous to and sometimes overlapping the mundane world. They were not alone in their faith, for every indigenous primal culture shares a belief in complementary realities, though their details are localized according to the country.

Modern, Western society still carries the legacy of the Age of Reason which, aided and abetted by the Industrial Revolution, firmly banished all faeries, spirits and 'irrational' states into a rationalist's oblivion. Most of us have consequently grown up to distrust that which we cannot see, to take faery and folk tales with a pinch of salt and to treat any personal impressions of complementary reality as signs of hallucination, mental breakdown or incipient madness.

The Celtic Otherworld exists as a complementary reality that can be visited. Its existence does not threaten or negate mundane reality, but co-exists alongside it. There are many aspects of the Otherworld, some of which we shall be exploring in this book (*see* Chapter Six). The Land of Faery is a name most commonly used by Celtic peoples nowadays to talk about the Otherworld. Faery can be both a place and an inhabitant of that place. Faeries are not diminutive beings with butterfly wings as depicted by Victorian romantics; they are the lordly ones, beings of great power, generally of greater stature than ourselves. One of the effects of travelling between mundane and otherworldly reality is the way in which things grow or diminish in stature, a feature explored in Lewis Carroll's *Alice in Wonderland*, a clever, though non-traditional look into the realms of Faery.

The original Faeries are the ancient deities of the Celtic world who were themselves symbolic expressions of the natural world. The Celts did not generally make images of their deities, preferring to venerate the sacred locus associated with the gods' power: springs, groves, wells, trees, mountains and estuaries were their natural temples. Certain parts of the land were memorable because of the great deeds done there and story-tellers in Ireland developed a genre of story called the *dindsenchas* or 'stories about the place'. The earth was held as sacred because it was 'deeply infused with mythic activity, invisible to mortal sight but perceptible to seers and storytellers, who, in Celtic tradition, were the priests of the gods' (C. Matthews *Arthur and the Sovereignty of Britain*).

Sacred sites are often distinct gateways to the Otherworld. A mound, a standing stone or a secluded lake may act as a focus for otherworldly activity. Through these gateways have strayed many unwary people. Folk tradition is rife with reports of people who have come home late and wandered accidentally into Faery. Such people have only come out again if they exercise courtesy and carry iron, the metal inimical to Faeries. The Faeries themselves are fond of musicians and poets, and will willingly entertain such artists, teaching them new skills, tunes and rhymes. Those who have returned often find that time has slipped by in the mundane world, while they may have enjoyed only a couple of days in Faery.

The Otherworld is the storehouse of archetypes that inform and shape our own phenomenal world. For example, take the trees that grow all around us in our own world: in the Otherworld they grow perfectly, without blight or frost to kill them. They have a luminous life, which is stronger and 'more real'. Also, the music that we listen to in our world is but a shadow of music's enchantment in the Otherworld. The archetypal reality of Faery may be likened to Plato's notion of the archetypal realms whence all original forms proceed. This idea is also found in the Christian hermetic and philosophic writings of the Middle Ages; the archetypal realm was thought to be ruled by angelic beings who kept things in harmony. This is indeed the function of the Otherworld. It also leads us to consider another aspect that is extremely important in our own age: the harmony that should exist between the mundane world and the Otherworld.

We are very much aware of the threat to our planet from over-production, pollution and mismanagement of resources; what we fail to see is the terrible effect that this has upon other realities. The exchange of gifts works both ways: the Otherworld provides the archetypes for our world to utilize, as long as we guard and preserve those gifts, using them wisely. If we abuse otherworldly gifts and misuse archetypal resources, we risk closing the gates that connect our two worlds. At first, we might assume that our own world alone would be the loser, but we do not take into account the way the Otherworld learns from our own mortal experience. Many legends speak of otherworldly beings who come into the mundane realm to take on mortality and to taste its bitter-sweet experiences.

The ever-present reality of the Otherworld is contactable through many means of which we are already aware: important dreams inform us of complementary reality, though we are seldom skilled enough to read and understand what we dream. We can re-create the Otherworld through narrative and through visualitive meditation, which we will be discovering in Chapter Six.

As stated above, Celtic story-tellers, poets and musicians – the descendants of the druids, bards and ovates of the ancient Celts – preserved the otherworldly traditions by their art. The traditional story-tellers – called *seanachies* in Ireland, or *cyfarwyddion* in Wales – preserved genres of story, each with its own magical spell. The oral memory of the Celts was impressive even by the standards of non-literate societies. The memorization of 250 prime stories and 100 secondary stories was part of the curriculum of a Celtic poet in her twelve-year training period. After the conquest of the Celtic realms, these stories were zealously retained and passed down to worthy recipients.

A remark of St Patrick about a story called *The House of the Two Goblets* is intriguing. He says that no-one should sleep or talk during this story and 'that it should not be told save at the prayer of good people who were worthiest to hear it' (C.M. Löffler). This may lead us to believe that only certain people were allowed to hear it and that it was passed down by a small band of story-tellers initiated into the blessings attached to this story:

> If thou repeatest the story of Ethne
> (the heroine of the tale)
> when taking a stately wife
> good is the step thou takest,
> thou shalt have the best of wives and children.
> . . . Repeat to a wealthy king
> the story of Ethne during destruction
> he will not lose his throne
> if he listens in silence.
> If you repeat this wondrous story
> to the prisoners of Ireland
> . . . they will be freed of their fetters . . . (ibid).

Such blessings are commonly attached to the different genres of stories, which were frequently recited at appropriate moments in life. The story of a battle (*cath*), for example, would be told before a battle, a birth-story of a hero (*compert*) at the occasion of a lying-in, a death-tale (*aided*) at a wake, etc.

This 'blessing of the story' can hardly be appreciated by us today, so exposed are we to instant entertainment at the turn of a button. The experience of listening to an oral story in complete silence – so as not to distract the story-teller's concentration – is one we infrequently enjoy.

As the story unfolded, the mind's eye of the listener was filled with images and subtle allusions. Story-tellers were people of great skill, attuned to the inner meaning of the story; it was this attunement that communicated itself to the listener and made the story-telling an occasion of magical empowerment. Story-telling was usually an evening occupation or reserved for the dead weeks of winter when there was little work to do on the land. It is interesting to note that story-tellers practised their art only at night. When Jeremiah Curtin, a nineteenth-century folklorist and story-collector went about County Kerry in Ireland collecting stories, he revisited a famous *seanachie*, an old woman, who said that she had been hospitalized since his last visit. She blamed this on the fact that she had been telling him (mainly ghost and faery) stories during the daytime. The Irish proscription on daytime story-telling may have been to do with upholding the appropriate nature of the story: the best time for otherworldly contact is after twilight. Another reason may be that, when stories were told, the Faeries were said to stop work and listen: as the Faeries helped humans maintain mundane tasks, this would have been unfortunate!

Story-tellers and bards often travelled in circuits, moving around the land and being maintained by patrons. Other *seanachies* were permanently attached to socially-important households. Today, in parts of Gaelic Scotland and Ireland, the story-teller's house may also be the *Ceilidh* house, where the community comes of an evening to hear stories, make music and sing songs.

The story-teller would take up residence in a settlement and the people would gather together in the largest room to listen for maybe four to eight nights while the story unfolded. Adults and children old enough to be quiet would be exposed to the story-teller's art and be able to share the exploits of heroes and heroines, and to enter the Otherworld with them. These stories were not told for mere recreational entertainment in the same way we watch television; they communicated traditional lore, showing young people ways of appropriate behaviour, giving older people insights into wise ways of counsel, and enabling all to meet the complementary realities of the Otherworld within a safe framework. The stories were recitals wherein natural laws were imparted. In pre-Christian society, the story-teller was therefore a guardian who imparted moral rectitude and right behaviour to his or her listeners.

This work of initiatory story-telling is also apparent in the mystery teachings of the ancient world; in Greece, for example, the rites of Eleusus were presented in a dramatic format, with the candidates for initiation enacting the main parts of the gods. In Celtic countries, not all people were exposed to the mystical training of bards and druids, but all were able to listen and understand the stories that underpinned the spiritual traditions. This is why Christianity was so readily accepted among the Celts: the missionaries following in their Saviour's footsteps used the oral tradition of story-telling to communicate the Christian mysteries. The parables of the Gospel fell onto fertile soil and were speedily assimilated with earlier pagan traditions to create the spiritual wealth of the Celtic Church. Many early accounts speak of Christ in terms of a Celtic hero: his wondrous *compert* or conception by the Blessed Virgin, his *macgnimartha* or youthful exploits in the temple at Jerusalem, his *slugard* or hosting in the gathering of his disciples, and his fearful *aided* or death tale at the Crucifixion. These were themes readily comprehensible to the Celtic temperament.

The story-teller acted as a guardian of otherworldly traditions, revealing the inner meanings through skilled retelling. Along these established pathways, seekers were enabled to explore their own problems and frustrations in a creative way, finding empowerment and help in time of trouble. It is to the source of the 'saving story' that we too are drawn today: people find the companionship of the story in scriptures, poetry and novels, for these may reveal deep wells of nourishment in times of need. I do not speak here of recreational reading only, although that too may play its part, but of the stories to which we turn when our back is against the wall, when facing isolation or stress. There is no greater healing than to be told a story that answers our present condition or predicament. Each of us has a story to which we can respond whole-heartedly and which will teach us wisdom. The repetition and 'giving' of that story may provide us with clues about the purpose and direction of our own life, as well as imparting initiatory teaching to others.

An example of this kind of story is the Maelduin Voyage, which is the subject of this book. The method I have used to uncover it may be used with many other stories in similar ways. Each story has its inherent wisdom that will strike us differently each time we read or hear it. We have read above how certain genres of story would be told at critical moments in life: the story of the otherworldly voyage or *immram* would be recited before setting out to sea. I also believe that it had other uses, such as being recited to people who were preparing for death. Its modern uses extend to the times when we each stand at decisive crossroads in our life, when we enter the borderlands of uncertainty, when we face a difficult passage from one mode of being to another. It is to this genre of *immram* that we turn next, in order to appreciate the wisdom that lies within it.

VOYAGES TO OTHERWORLDS

The tradition of the *immram* is based upon certain fundamental understandings: the voyage enacts the passing into the Otherworld, the testing of the soul, the passage into and beyond death and the empowerment of the spiritual quest. In Celtic tradition two factors are constant: the Otherworld lies across water; and the direction taken by the voyage is generally to the West. The West is often perceived as the place of the dead in mythology. The ancient Egyptians saw the western bank of the Nile as the abode of the dead. In English colloquial parlance we say something has 'gone West', meaning it has become dysfunctional. In Celtic countries, the Isles of the Blessed – the otherworldly abodes – lie to the West. Here can be found the great mysteries of the gods and the empowering objects of the spiritual quest: immortality, otherworldly gifts and spiritual teachings.

Water in the form of rivers, lakes and springs was venerated by the Celts as the abode of the Goddess who fed the land's fertility. But the sea was the 'Great Water', the most dangerous of all, since to cross it was to trust entirely in the gods of the elements. The traditional Celtic folk-song often reflects this theme:

> The water is wide, I cannot cross o'er,
> And neither have I wings to fly,
> Bring me a boat that can carry two,
> And I will sail, my love, to you.

In most mythic traditions, the sea is symbolic of the originating element of life, of the abyss, the cauldron of creation from which we derive. To return purposefully to the sea and take a voyage of discovery is a significant act of recapitulation, a return to the womb of the mother in order to be reborn or mystically transformed.

In ancient megalithic tradition, the ship appears as a feminine image, frequently having upon it a tree of life, an ankh or a serpent – all symbols of renewal. We still name boats after women; and the Mediterranean tradition of painting the 'eye of Her' (the Goddess) upon either side of the prow is still current. Figure-heads of Goddesses, which adorned the prows of ocean-going vessels in the eighteenth century and earlier, are reminiscent of Odysseus' personal guidance by Athene in Homer's *Odyssey*. In Celtic tradition, an otherworldly woman from the Island of Women invites the traveller to take an *immram* and acts as a protector and guide on the voyage, in keeping with this ancient tradition.

Death and the sea are closely associated in Celtic tradition. Votive boats have been found, sometimes fashioned of gold, in north Wales and at Broighter in County Derry, Northern Ireland. Here we see the ship as chariot of the sun. In Corco Duibne in south-western Ireland, which has an unparalleled view of the setting sun over the Atlantic Ocean, it is said that the Goddess Mor is on her throne. Mor is one of the names given to the Queen of the Land of Women, to which many pilgrims voyage.

The association of death and the sea is further borne out in Irish wake customs, one of which was recorded in the last century. The game of 'The Building of the Ship' was played at Irish wakes by men and youths, involving much horseplay and ribaldry. It comprised several scenes, the first of which was the 'laying the keel', where youths were laid on their backs in a row, and the master of ceremonies walked over them with his attendants, tapping them with his staff to see if the 'timber' was sound. Next came the 'placing the stem and stern posts' scene. Two youths were put at either end of the keel sitting upright; then a double row of youths, the first line lying down, the second seated facing inwards on either side of the keel made the ribs and sides. Again the master would walk down the row of legs, kicking them to test the workmanship. The 'painting of the ship' involved getting a bucket of dirty water and a mop, and pouring the water over the performers. The 'erecting the mast' saw the youngest boy placed centrally as the mast. Many expressive gestures and acts were part of this section of the game, but are now lost to us, probably because of the nature of the game: all the men were naked during this performance. When the 'erecting the mast' was mentioned to an old man by a folklorist in the nineteenth century, he said: 'Lord, how did you know that? It's nearly sixty years since I saw it, and sure the priests wouldn't let it be acted now' (Wood-Martin). The juxtaposition of ribald games with death may seem peculiar to us, but it seems to have been an ancient feature of northern-European culture, and can be found depicted in Scandinavian Bronze-Age stone engravings. Many ships and ithyphallic figures are depicted on these stones. North-west Europe also has a tradition of ship burials, where the dead were set adrift on a boat that was then burned. Sometimes the ship was interred, such as at Sutton Hoo in East Anglia, England.

The sixth-century Greek historian, Procopius, writes of the ship that ferries the dead souls between Brittany and Cornwall, which unwary fishermen are called upon to pilot. The ship grows heavy as the souls board it, but it lightens when they disembark (Patch).

The *immrama* stories are complementary to these traditions. The earliest *immram* is that of Bran mac Febal, transcribed in the seventh century. This begins when Bran is alone: unearthly music sends him into a deep sleep and he awakes to find a silver branch beside him, blossoming with crystal flowers. In the middle of the locked house, a woman of the Otherworld appears and sings to him of the wonders of the land from which she comes:

Unknown is wailing or treachery in the well-cultivated land ... there is no sickness, grief, sorrow or death there. In the house of

silver jewels and crystals rain, and where the sea washes wave on land, drops of crystal shake from its mane.

She tells him of the marvels that await there and exhorts Bran to 'make a voyage across the clear sea to see if you can reach the Land of Women' (Patch). The silver branch flies from his hand to hers and Bran sets sail with three companies of nine men, each captained by one of his three foster-brothers. They meet the sea god Manannan mac Lír who tells Bran of his wonderful undersea realm:

Since creation we have not aged or decayed; we are never sick, for we are free from sin.

He prophesies about Bran's coming to Ireland where he will engender the hero Mongan. (Irish tradition has many colourful stories concerning the half-immortal Mongan who, like many another hero, lives but a short – if glorious – time. The comings of Mongan and Christ are juxtaposed in the *Voyage of Bran* poem, suggesting the hand of a cleric who saw the overlapping of the pagan and Christian traditions.) Bran continues rowing until he and his company find the Land of Women where they remain for many years until one man suffers homesickness. The Queen of the Land of Women warns them not to touch Irish soil. They sail to Ireland where Bran hails a man on the shore and asks for news. The man is astounded because the voyage of Bran is for him an ancient legend. The homesick voyager leaps ashore and immediately crumbles to dust. Bran then returns to the Land of Women, nevermore to set sail for home.

We note that in this story the *immram* is accelerated or triggered by a vision of an otherworldly woman who is the bringer of dreams or a messenger from the Land of Women. The motivation for the *immram* is not very clear and this may be due to the fragmentary nature of the text.

The next *immram*, that of Maelduin, will be considered in full detail in Chapter Two. From it derive many other *immrama*, including the *Voyage of Snedgus and Mac Riagla*, transcribed in the tenth century, which starts as a voyage for vengeance against an enemy. The heroes discover many islands inhabited by heavenly wonders. The *Voyage of Ua Corra's Boat*, probably eleventh century in date, follows the adventures of the sons of Corra who take their *immram* as a journey of repentance for youthful bad deeds. It is a rather dull ecclesiastical *immram* designed to edify the ungodly and, like other *immrama*, draws upon the Maelduin voyage rather heavily.

The most famous *immram* of all is the *Navigatio Sancti Brendani*, or *Voyage of St Brendan*. In this story, St Brendan (489–?583) hears the tales of St Barrind who had taken a recent *immram* to the Promised Land of Saints. Brendan sets out with fourteen monks on a similar voyage. The course of his *immram* is almost identical to that of Maelduin and is clearly based upon it. Some notable variant incidents include the celebration of mass upon the back of a whale, the visit to a fully operational Celtic monastery and an encounter with Judas. St Brendan sails within sight of the Promised Land of Saints but is unable to cross the river. Brendan returns and records his *immram*.

Notably absent from Brendan's story is a visit to the Land of Women. Indeed, we might believe that his world was populated by nothing but men, for not even holy virgins inhabit these islands; the only woman in the *immram* appears to them in bird-shape, a fate decreed by God for her sins.

These brief glimpses at the *immrama* tradition barely hint at its rich variety. They do show us, however, that the *immram* constitutes a voyage of adventure, danger and often translation into another state, such as in Maelduin's *immram*, when Diurán is renewed in body, or when Maelduin's foster-brother enters the Island of Joy. What lies beyond the uttermost West is death and transformation. The function of the *immram* is to teach the craft of dying, to pilot the departing soul over a sea of perils and wonders. But it can also be a method of exploring better ways of living so that, by exposure to the dangers of the unknown and by overcoming perils, the soul may be rekindled and attuned to its true purpose.

There was provision in Celtic law for offenders to be tested by the elements and set adrift in a small boat without oars or rudder, with only a bailer and a knife. If they were washed ashore, it was considered that they had been sufficiently purified by the gods; if they drowned, then that was their allotted fate.

The idea of a journey to seek transformation or purification occurs in tradition world-wide. We are familiar with the idea of pilgrimage as expiation, whereby pilgrims expose themselves to dangers in order to arrive at a sacred destination and make a rededication of themselves. Jerusalem was one of the most popular pilgrimage destinations for Western Christians, while Russian Christians would pilgrimage to the River Jordan. Moslems still make their *haj* to Mecca and Medina, while Sikhs journey to the Golden Temple at Amritsar. Even secular weekend holiday breaks may be regarded as pilgrimage, since they seek to transform or re-create the traveller (Sheldrake). Historically, many would-be pilgrims had neither means nor opportunity to seek out far-distant holy places, and had to content themselves with more local manifestations such as the maze at Chartres which, if traversed on the knees while in a state of grace, corresponded to a pilgrimage to Jerusalem.

The expiatory voyage or journey of self-discovery very often takes place within such a microcosmic context in Celtic spiritual tradition. Rather than the actual voyage, pilgrims learn the lessons of an *immram*; rather than suffering in purgatory, they make the arduous climb of Croagh Patrick or fast from food and sleep for three days upon St Patrick's Purgatory.

St Patrick's Purgatory is located on Station Island in Lough Derg, County Donegal, Eire. Here, thousands of barefoot Catholic pilgrims come each year to suffer the comfortless penance of prayer and fasting upon this rocky island. The barefoot climb of Croagh Patrick in County Mayo, Eire, is enacted yearly in remembrance of St Patrick's forty-day fast during Lent, since the tradition says that here, as at St Patrick's Purgatory, the penitent may thus avoid suffering in the Christian Otherworld.

Such expiatory pilgrimages are not the sole preserve of the Christian tradition. Spirit-voyaging by means of a boat is a common feature of shamanic traditions world-wide. The Big Canoe or Spirit Canoe is a feature of native American legend, a correlative to the Celtic boat without oar or rudder, and the glass boat of Irish tradition piloted by Manannan, God of the Otherworld. The boat has always been symbolic of that frail bark, the soul, which sails across the seas of life and beyond.

The tradition of voyages of self-discovery range from Homer's *Odyssey* to Samuel Taylor Coleridge's *The Rime of the Ancient Mariner*. The perennial popularity of these stories is testimony to the reader's identification with the lone voyager, adrift and at the mercy of the gods and elements. These voyages are still being re-created in works of fiction. *The Voyage of the Dawn Treader*, from C.S. Lewis's Narnia series, tells the story of King Caspian's voyage to the uttermost East. It is a book firmly based in the *immrama* tradition. Even Gene Roddenbury's television series *Star Trek* may be seen as an *immram* through the heavens in its search for new life forms and galactic information. J.R.R. Tolkien's *The Lord of the Rings* has Frodo's final voyage to the Grey Havens of the Elves, identifiably parallel to the Celtic Blessed Islands.

It is upon the never-ending sea of our own lives that we each make a voyage of discovery to find ourselves and to understand our own *immram*.

St Brendan the Navigator is shown here, landing on an island that turns out to be a whale, in this fifteenth-century woodcut.

the Voyage of Maelduin

*Someone will remember my song in every generation;
my story will not be forgotten if you remember it.*

Song of Fothad Canainne

The *immram* upon which this *Celtic Book of the Dead* is based is *Immram Curaig Maelduin Inso* or *The Voyage of Maelduin's Boat*. This text was transcribed in the eighth or ninth century, although later transcriptions exist. Apart from the *Voyage of Bran*, it is the earliest *immram* story. Many incidents in the *Voyage of St Brendan* are reworkings of scenarios found in the Maelduin story.

There are many learned editions of the text, but for the purposes of this book I have chosen to work from H.P.A. Oskamp's edition (Groningen, 1970). The original language of the story is Old Irish, the ancestor of the modern Irish Gaelic language that is still spoken in the *Gaeltacht* (Irish-speaking) areas of Eire. The prose narrative is interspersed with a poetic summary, possibly written by Aed Finn, a poet and sage about whom we have no further information.

This chapter begins with my own translation of the full text of this poem, in order to give the true flavour of the original *immram*. It is followed by a shortened prose retelling of the *Voyage of Maelduin* and accompanied by a commentary intended to clarify unfamiliar expressions and concepts. In the poem and the commentary, I have given each island a title descriptive of its quality; these titles are not found in the original text. I have striven to bring out the nature of the experience that underlies each island encounter; this has been equated with the journey taken through life as well as with the inner voyage that specialist voyagers, such as shamans, take to understand further the interconnected nature of the many-coloured worlds. There is more discussion of the shamanic tradition and its correlations with the *immrama* in Chapter Six.

It is hard to say whether the prose narrative predates the poetic summary. The crafts of the poet and story-teller in ancient Ireland were intermingled to such a degree that it is possible that story and poem grew out of each other. A marginal addition to the text tells us: 'Now Aed Finn, chief sage of Ireland, arranged this story as it stands here; and he did so for delighting the mind and for the people of Ireland after him' (Oskamp). Considering the advice to the reciter that is given at the end of the poem: 'Sing seven verses before (its recital), then read ten (stanzas): this is the noblest recitation', we may be led to believe that Aed Finn's intention was that each part of the poem was to act as a summary to the prose narration which may have been told in a staggered, sequential manner. The fact that the story was arranged at all leads us to suppose that it was orally extant.

Whatever the original intention of Aed Finn might have been, we are left with a stunning and unforgettable sequence of otherworldly encounters in which Maelduin sails into the furthest West and finds his destiny. It is from the many islands of this story that the *immram* cards are derived.

In approaching the text, my method has been to set it in its original historical and social context as much as possible, without resort to modern metaphors or images. My prose retelling is shorter than the original text, often summarizing longer conversations or descriptive passages, in order to provide the reader with a clear story-line. I have chosen to translate the whole of the Maelduin poem as closely as possible. The style of the poem is terse and often laconically amusing. I have made few rationalizations of its exceedingly concise statements, choosing instead to explain these in either footnotes to the poem or later in the commentary to the story. This translation attempts to represent the dense and lapidary style of the Irish poet or *filé*, although the assonantal quality of the Irish has been replaced here by an English alliteration.

Readers should note that the poem and the story vary slightly from each other in certain details. These variations may have arisen as a result of divergent oral traditions being transcribed in the arrangement of Aed Finn, or they may have happened as the result of an inattentive copyist.

the Poem

HERE BEGINS THE STORY OF MAELDUIN'S VOYAGE.

The noble, High King of Heaven, World's Creator, in every time and place, be our assistance!

Many beautiful places are there upon earth, gracious their appearance; however we enumerate them, their virtue is clear.

*The Son has spoken of the Father's many mansions, he has successively stripped the bark of revelation, in each age of the many-coloured world.

Plenteous were the wonders upon the blue wave's kingdom; swift was the sailing when Maelduin made his voyaging.

Maelduin was the son of Ailill of the Battle's Height: a great warrior was he, fierce, implacable, generous.

†The lord of Ninuss went hosting, a star-led destiny; Ailill went with him, with high courage, with fierce ardour.

Though high-spirited youths incited Ailill, he kept to his lord's company. A nun came forth to ring the bell.

Ardent Ailill overpowered her like a strong man; of their embraces was born Maelduin, the noble champion.

In secret was he raised by a kindly foster-mother. As a beardless boy, he was handsome and striking in appearance.

---

* Here the many islands of the *immram* are compared with the saying of Christ: 'In my Father's house are many rooms . . . I go to prepare a place for you' (John 14.2).
† Bands of warriors 'went hosting', gathering together to go on warlike forays or cattle-reeving expeditions. Hosting was usually a seasonal activity.

A rash warrior taunted him sorely, after a victorious ball game, right before
those who had lost the game.
Said the man: 'No sure or noble paternity is yours, no land are you
possessed of, no mother of humankind bore you.'
Thereupon, his kind foster-mother led him to his mother, the nun; and
after hearing of Ailill's death, Maelduin went to search out his kinfolk.
But the bitter taunt of Briccne was ever the goad to avenge the death of his
wealthy father, Ailill, upon those who murdered him.
He went then to the deep druid of Corcomruadh for his wise counsel, that
he might know the augury.
*Into the sea's tumult scudded his three-skinned ship; and with favourable
wind, he sailed from Ireland.
But his crew flouted the druid's counsel, taking on board the three foster-
brothers of Maelduin: a journey of sorrowful toil was theirs.
†The ship sailed hardily to an island wherein warriors boasted shamelessly
of killing Ailill.
Then rose a wind, blowing from the shore, a rough wind blew them away,
a serpentine course over the seal-strewn ocean of the West.
‡Beyond the ninth wave their dark ship drifted, over the crested kingdom
of the deep to the habitation of the islanded West.

i ISLAND OF GIANT ANTS

A swarm of ants the size of foals approached them on the first island. Their
course awry, their way unsure.

---

* Maelduin sets out in a skin-covered boat or curragh. Such simple, though smaller, boats are still used by fishermen on the Aran Islands today.
† This island does not appear in our *immram* since it belongs to the earthly realm. Maelduin finds it again at the end of his voyage.
‡ The ninth wave was considered to be the magical boundary of the land, beyond which was another country. In ancient times, boats usually hugged coastlines rather than venturing on the open sea.

2 ISLAND OF MANY BIRDS

To an island they sailed to find great but gentle birds, abundantly settled on
   terraces in many thousands.
They laded the ship with them, swift was their passage; this island pleasant
   after their journeying, a wondrous passage.

3 ISLAND OF THE HOUND-FOOTED HORSE

A great beast it was, a dog the size of a high-stepping horse; they soon
   decided their best course was swift retreat.

4 ISLAND OF INVISIBLE RIDERS

Another island was sighted — not before time — but the sight of it gripped
   their hearts with terror.
Two warriors went to essay the sharp terrain, scoured with hoof-prints; all
   was prepared for a race-meeting, it seemed.
But the size of the cups like cauldrons — an honourable quaffing that! — the
   hoof-prints, each as large as a sail, and a race-meeting readied. . .
They fled in anguished retreat, a deed without valour; swiftly and unseen
   came beings to the sea-shore race.
They had their race, upraised voices in shouts of encouragement; the crew
   perceived by the dust that here was a hosting of spirits.

5 ISLAND OF PLENTEOUS SALMON

They came to a hostel, richly and nobly appointed; in its door a valve of
   slick stone — a bright dwelling there.
Towards the sea was a broad and ample door; it was marvellous the way
   the white green-speckled wave threw in the sound, tasty fish.
Within that house was a carven bed for each three men, vessels of crystal
   wherein wondrous liquor companioned the abundant food.

A soft chair was set for the swift Maelduin, a deed of kinship; good was the feasting within that fair house.

*Liquor flowing from crystal cups, the food that each desired; their swift brown boat skimmed the wild waves.

6 ISLAND OF TREES

Such was the island to which they came over the watery wave, its tall shade cast by a copse of tangled trees.

Our praiseworthy hero broke one slight stem; his ship cruised onwards, its sails filled with song not storm-winds.

Three days following, at the stem's tip — no mean feat this — our hero found a great treasure, three apples flourishing.

Three rounds of forty days and nights, they satisfied the ship's company with these apples' admirable sweetness.

It robbed them of sharp hunger pangs, kept their thirst quenched; it brought the vigour of gentle drunkenness to each stout fellow.

7 ISLAND OF THE REVOLVING BEAST

They saw a steep island over the ocean's heaving, whereon a great beast performed an entertaining feat:

It stretched itself, vigorously revolving its bones within its loose skin; it made a great noise on the high-placed rock.

It ran swiftly over the island, in a circuit of careering, till it performed its feat of revolving inside its skin.

Swiftly it reared from side to side, revolving recklessly; our generous, fair-haired warriors took to sea, without any turning themselves!

---

* The Holy Grail also dispenses the food that is most desired; Grail legends often draw upon otherworldly elements.

It cast showers of stones to injure them; so they left that wondrous land to
the mighty beast.

8 ISLAND OF CANNIBAL HORSES

In another island, a herd of strong but wretched beasts with grinding teeth:
their feats were bloody.

9 ISLAND OF FIERY PIGS

They neared an island with a wood of excellent fruits; apples of gold, their
scent exquisite.

Clod-like beasts gorge on them, on the sweet-smelling apples of the sea-girt
island.

Filled to satiety, they go underground in the afternoon, when flocks of
white sea-borne birds fly in for their fill.

Thick was the air over that island because of the great heat; the pigs turn
constantly and scratch their haunches.

The crew took many apples from that land, so that the swift crooked ship
was full after their visiting.

10 ISLAND OF THE CAT

The next island had a high paling of swan's whiteness. Within was a noble
hall, a king's fit dwelling:

Brooches of silver, gold-hilted swords, wide necklets, soft beds, sweet food
and golden benches.

Nourishing was the sweet feast there, health-giving liquor; above it was a
quick hungry cat poised on a pillar.

It leapt between pillars, a speedy feat: a diminutive steward for the feast,
yet not appalling.

One of the foster-brothers of our powerful chieftain, filled with daring, took
    a gold necklace weighing a good ounce.
The wondrous cat's fiery paw rent his body, the guilty corpse of the
    wretched one consumed to ash.
The necklace was fetched back again, friendship was restored: the ashes of
    the wretched wight cast into the ocean.

11 ISLAND OF BLACK AND WHITE

Three days later they came to an island, without fear or danger; a wall of
    brass, pleasant to see, divided it.
Large flocks grazed on either side: one black flock here, one white flock
    there – a wonder of the world.
There was a man with an intricate crook in his hand; he performed a
    wondrous feat with the two flocks.
He would throw a white sheep among the black flock, so that it became
    black; then he would throw a black sheep among the white flock, so
    that it became white.
With black and white wands, swiftly found, did they try the ground, a
    baffling trick.
Black among white has the swan's colour, a white fair body; white among
    black has the colour of coal, each wand their answerer.

12 ISLAND OF GIANT CATTLE

They rowed to an island upon their way, where Diurán of the fair palm, the
    sweet-tongued poet, saw a deep, narrow river.
It melted the shaft of his blue spear, a fierce dissolution; on the far side
    beneath a rock were black-legged oxen.

He banged spear on shield to frighten them; a great barrel of a man crossed
    him completely.
'Why do you worry the little calves?' said he. 'Without boasting,' said
    Diurán, 'tell me where are the cattle that threw these calves?'
'Any who wish to know that may journey over the mountain to see that
    the dams outdo their offspring.'
Brave Diurán returned over the waves; he brought the best pig from the
    large herd he found there.
They soon did for that pig, the crew of that curragh; then they went
    onward over the turbulent waves.

13 ISLAND OF THE MILL

The next island to which they came over the glittering sea had a mill upon
    it, fearful its aspect.
A grudging miller stood guard there; from east to west, each grudged
    burden went between the wheels.
They asked the miller, for they saw none greater, whence came the loads
    that the rich throng brought to him?
'From your own country the host is dragging its burden: the mill retains
    only the debts of ungenerosity.'

14 ISLAND OF SORROW

They found an island whereon a twisting throng of sorrowful people
    turned; they sent one man to inquire without affront.
He asked the mourners what made them mourn; then he wept to swell the
    torrent of tears; he joined their lamentation.
The one who had been sent, chosen by lot — unwillingly was that passage —
    was gentle foster-brother to Maelduin, of that boat's kinship.

Two strong men were sent to him, to take him away; but though they did
    not delay in their errand, they too fell to wailing.
Then came four others, with caution and trepidation; the two were saved,
    with good fortune; but the foster-brother was taken care of in that
    place.

15 ISLAND OF THE FOUR FENCES

They came to another island, brought by the clear, swift waters, in which a
    noble company was set.
Four divisions were upon that island, without guile or reproach: maidens,
    warriors of certain victory, kings and queens.
Four palisades divided the island: strong brass, noble silver, fair crystal and
    the ridged red gold.
Of wondrous brass, of shining crystal — who can believe it? — with smooth
    structure as by a blacksmith flattened.
A white-skinned shapely maiden came to them; of excellent hospitality,
    graceful beauty and noble spirit.
The girl brought them cheese, the food of their desire; she portioned it out
    — this excellent gift — with health-giving drink.
On the third day, that island had vanished; so they went out to sea, a long
    course, occasioned by need.

16 ISLAND OF THE CRYSTAL KEEP

They rowed towards a small island on which was a stout fortress; around it
    a strong brass fence made a good defence.
Around the fence, too wonderful for telling, was a still moat of beauty; a
    bridge of glass was before it.

Our swift, proud warriors of renown stepped often upon it, to be thrown

down backwards – a singular and repetitive homage!

They saw approaching a white-necked woman attired in a robe of swan's
brilliance, a woman of wisdom and fair deeds.

About her white mantle an edging of red gold, delightfully lustrous; upon
her feet sandals of silver – a singular casing!

Her mantle was fastened by a brooch of fair silver, with twisted gold work,
fine craftsmanship.

Yellow locks of golden hue hung from her head, her going was gracious,
royal was her stately mien.

Beneath the fair bridge, like a holy place, was hidden a well of pure water, a
stout well-cover over it.

The beautiful and greatly favoured woman was busy pouring out draughts
of the invigorating liquid, without offering them any – a strange action.

Loud-mouthed German spoke fittingly to her: 'We are astounded not to be
offered hospitality.'

For answer she left them, barring the noble rath to them; its cross-slashed
door sang sweet, harmonious melody that night.

The chorus of singing brought sleep to their eyes as she preordained; on
the morrow, the woman returned unabashed.

So it continued until the third day, three days without feasting with the
good woman's music to soothe them.

She brought them into that spacious dwelling over the wild ocean, a good
square meal she gave them, with sweet-tasting liquor.

The busy noblewoman without any evil intention, without error of any
kind, uttered the name of each of them.

When she was asked to lie with their leader and meet his desire, she replied
that she was one who did not know guile.

'You do not speak according to your heart, your words follow not your faith; but so that I may reveal the secret of the island to you, inquire of me.'

When they awoke that morrow they were within their boat, none knew the whereabouts of that noble island.

17 ISLAND OF SINGING BIRDS

North of the ocean they heard a sound of a courageous gathering, only softly like the singing of harmonious choirs.

They came over the blue ocean, wearied of their immram, until they reached an island of wondrous birds.

18 ISLAND OF THE ANCESTORS

Upon a small island, they found a psalming ancient; his noble mien was full of dignity, holy were his words.

The hair of his head made a bright cloak, a white garment was his, a sparkling mantle; waves of whiteness wrapped about him.

Our high chieftain asked, 'Whence come you?' 'I will not conceal what you ask me – from the land of the Gaels.

'My pilgrimage led me over the pelting seas, without my boat bursting asunder; I did not regret going.

'Then my crooked curragh split under me upon the boiling sea; a salt and sudden wave lifted me shorewards.

'I cut a turf from the grey-green land of my ancestors; a sea-breeze blew me to the place I am in now, though it was compassed narrowly.

*'Then did the star-strong King make broad an island from the little wondrous sod, of sea-gull's hue its shore-line.

* The star-strong King refers to Christ who, in Celtic tradition, is often addressed as 'King of the Elements'.

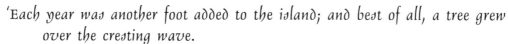

'Each year was another foot added to the island; and best of all, a tree grew
     over the cresting wave.

'A pure well fountained for me with eternal sustenance; by the protection
     of angels, sweet food, a sacred celebration.

'Each of you will come homeward, a fruitful company over the wave's
     track; a long journey though, except for one man.'

By the protecting angels, each man received a single half-loaf; with a kingly
     portion of fish each was furnished.

19 ISLAND OF THE HERMIT

Three full days following, they went into the body of the boat; the ebbing
     shallows took on a gladsome course.

Over the crested wave they saw an island cinctured with a golden wall; its
     gentle centre downy, though it was good ground for gathering.

In the middle was an ancient man in a white garment; his hair curled down
     his back, a wondrous sight.

Our noble leader asked him: 'Who provides your food?' 'From God comes
     my fair provision, a sacred celebration.

'Beside me is a clean well, my kingly ruler; it supplies me with food
     without stint.

'On feast-days it gives sweet whey, ale on Sundays; on the days of martyrs
     it gives no scanty portion, but plenteous and without stint.

'On the feasts of apostles, on the days of John and Mary, quantities of good
     ale does it give, invigorating liquor of lasting warmth.

'Wine it gives on the solemnities of the High King of Creation, Jesus the
     noble abbot, Son of Mary.'

Half a loaf and a portion of fish; sweet food for three days without stint
     was given them on that island.

THE VOYAGE OF MAELDUIN

20 ISLAND OF THE FORGE

They took their way over the smooth-faced seas to an island wherein they
found fearful smiths.

Said a strong active smith from the door of his forge: 'I see a strange and
noble immram over the brilliant seas.

'A company of young men rowing over the mighty sea in a trough; swift is
their rowing, a wondrous band swinging together.'

*'Row the boat backwards,' bawled our leader. A successful effort, they
moved away over the flaming sea.

When they saw their swift retreat, the smiths staggered after them in
furious pursuit.

One ran speedily, seizing the great tongs with a clot of iron, the ruthless
one; he ran vigorously in great leaps.

The sea boiled from that hot iron; the ebbing tide took it: a deed to be
proclaimed.

21 SEA OF GLASS

They came to an utterly green sea of glass-like hue; they could see beneath
them – a mighty wealth – the stones of the sea.

22 SEA OF MIST

They rowed over the wondrous, cloud-like sea; beneath the keel, tall towers
all utterly silent.

In that country beneath was a bitter beast in a forking tree of great growth.

The sharp-finned beast, because of its appetite, took an adult ox before their
very eyes; the herd flew from it.

---

* Maelduin urges his men to row backwards, but not to turn the boat; this is so that the giant smith will assume they are still coming
towards the island, rather than retreating.

Then the strong herdsman fled more slowly, so that the beast might not strike him – a terrible thought!

23 ISLAND OF RECOGNITION

One of the wave's wonders was an eminent island, a fair house high above the sea's reaching.

The sea made an impenetrable wall about it; though they rowed around it, there was no welcome into that strong enclosure.

*The cries of a strong company of men came to them out of that pleasant plain, vehement their calling; a warlike host regarding them.

It seemed to our heroes that the host was like those who remembered a prophecy that they might one day be murdered in a sudden slaughter.

But a sweet, fair-haired woman began to cast sound nuts at them which they were able to take on their voyage – a freight more welcome than treasure.

24 ISLAND OF THE RAINBOW STREAM

From the nave of the boat, they saw a strange hard thing: a door of stone from which ran a stream of clear bright water.

Over the island in an arch it bent, no small drop, towards another fair door, in a bright stream.

Along that arching stream there leapt strong fish, headlong, their career piercing the stream.

But not on Sunday did that stream run, in singular homage to the holy day of resurrection.

They gathered many of those savoury fish before the swift waves rolled them into stormy waters.

* The pleasant plain, or Mag Mell meaning 'Plain of Honey', is one of the names for the Otherworld.

25 PILLAR OF THE SILVER NET

They rowed then towards something towering over them in the ocean; a
  strange but noble thing of bright silver lustre.

From a four-sided pillar's height hung a net of purest silver guarding the
  western plain of the sea.

*The ship sailed through the great net's mesh in swift strokes, and the
  powers were victorious.

A gentle voice of power spoke from the bright pillar, though no-one
  understood its utterance.

No-one could tell, though the voice was loud enough, whether it was
  human or some other power that uttered.

The indefatigable Diurán hacked off five ounces of the net, that the voyage
  might be believed.

Upon the altar of sweet-tongued Patrick the Victorious did he place it, that
  his deed might be upheld before the hosts.

26 ISLAND OF THE SHUTTERED DOOR

They journeyed to a strange island over the sea's rim; it stood on an iron
  foot, an awesome cliff and well defended.

Around the island rowed the scouts, but no entrance showed over the sea's
  spume.

From their sortie they supposed that the entrance must lie within the lower
  part of the iron foot, though it was not clear.

A plough was on it, with cattle and plenteous wealth; but while they called
  the inhabitants, no answer came.

---

* The powers referred to here are those of the otherworldly guardians. The pillar marks the entrance to the deepest spiral of the
Otherworld (see Chapter Six).

27 ISLAND OF WOMEN

The green-backed wave brought them over the calm sea to an island, with a
    mound and fortress full of folk.
Beautiful maidens dwelt therein, as they could see; the bath they tended
    was filled with the brightest water.
Their noble mother came on a swift horse to greet the travellers; after their
    bath, the ringletted, open-handed woman set all in readiness and said:
'All who dwell here will not die; rest unbounded, clothes of soft and gentle
    weave will be your portion.
'Since the death of the king, each day I go to judge the people; sufficient is
    our treasury in the service of noble folk.'
Each time homesickness drew them back to the seas, this fair woman
    fetched them back, never hiding the fortress from them.
She would throw a sticky clew at the hand of our captain, so that the exiled
    warrior was continually brought back to the shore.
Finally, they had to sever the hand of one traveller that she might not
    delay them; sorrowfully, the female host wept for those adrift on the
    endless wave.

28 ISLAND OF BERRIES

The growing seas set them on another island; here a fragrant forest grew,
    with fruits abounding.
The trees like willow grew in ranks, with berries on them, hard to find their
    match, big as the heads of men.
The lot fell upon Maelduin to taste the juice of this prodigious fruit; it cast
    him into peaceful slumbers, seasoned time of healing.
The others mixed the potent juice with water, making a satisfying repast, a
    cordial of wondrous power.

29 ISLAND OF THE EAGLE

They went by water, driven by gale, a time without food; here was no
    aimless sailing for they found another island.

In its midst a church, larger than surmise; an ancient hardy cleric was its
    only inhabitant.

The grey-haired priest gave welcome to our noble company; the men from
    the land of the Gael took communion and received his blessing.

*'Whence come you,' asked Maelduin of the cleric, 'tell us truly.' 'I am one
    of Brendan of Birr's people,' he said clearly.

The island stretched smooth to the eye, sweetly sound; in its midst was a
    lake, and many sheep within a paling.

From the sea swept a great eagle of fierce flight; branch in its talons, it
    landed by the lake verge.

Other fine birds stripped a wondrous tree, its branches imparting the virtue
    of redness to the waters.

Joyfully they greeted the wondrous eagle, the noblest of birds, valiantly
    come to that place.

†The great bird dived into the lake, its years unburdening; it rose again in
    youth's vigour, stronger than ever before.

Diurán the Storysmith also dived in; no rash leap this, his body remains in
    finest fettle, without loss of hair or teeth.

30 ISLAND OF JOY

They saw people on the plain in a fair island; they seemed accustomed to
    play and laugh without cessation.

---

* The hermit is from the foundation of the sixth-century saint, Brendan of Birr, the friend of St Columba of Iona.
† The renewal of the eagle in the lake is paralleled by Psalm 102.5: 'Your youth is renewed like the eagle's.' Here it is a symbol of the eternal restoration of the soul.

One traveller went to ask their purpose; but their great merriment was no
   cause of joy for him.
Chosen by lot from the sea by our swift champion: a fine and generous
   man, the son of his foster-mother.
He soon fell to their playing, a pleasant pastime, not knowing his own
   fellows; they were a people without purpose.
Heavy the fate of the three foster-brothers, succumbed to strife; not one to
   his gentle kinfolk came again.

31 ISLAND OF CIRCLED FIRE

They reached a strange island by a hard and lengthy journey; around it, in
   the sea's midst, was a high and powerful wall.
Charming that host, wealthy that tribe, the folk of the fortress; the fiery
   rampart swiftly revolving.
They saw beyond the rampart into a doorway, wherein they glimpsed a
   lovely house of bright beings, of high renown.
Mild folk, choice treasures, tall spear-racks, fine vessels, wrought goldwork,
   purple garments.
Though they glimpsed them feasting within without fear; they dared not
   penetrate the fiery harbour.

32 ISLAND OF OTTERS

They had rowed peaceful and happy for many a moon when the swift
   waters fetched them over the seas.
They saw a rock, a scalable cliff, and a man thereon: ill-framed he was,
   with only hair for a garment.
They boldly rowed towards him, exchanging kindly greetings and noble
   blessings.

'Whence came you to this place beyond the seas?' 'I am a cook who once
    dwelt on Tory.

'Great wealth was entrusted to me, it's the plain truth; easy it was to sell
    the brothers' food and line my pocket.

'So it was until I went to bury a dead brother; I heard a voice saying,
    "Bury not the sinner above my grave!

' "If you do this, your place will be in hell; if you desist, heaven will
    receive you when you die.

' "Test me, for this burial will abort." — No truer word, for the grave filled
    swiftly by itself with soil.

'Great was my thieving, I was a despoiler of my kind; pride and greed
    drove me to sea with a boat of plunder.

'While on the clear waters with all my spoils, I saw a cleric of shining
    countenance.

'He said, "Stay your course! Make truce with Heaven's King; the ocean
    surrounding you is full of beings on every side."

' "I'll do your bidding, fear not," said I. "Then cast aside your plunder into
    the deep cleansing seas.

' "Set your course away from shore, swift waves speed your sailing!" — He
    prophesied that I should be wherever my bark went under me.

'A cup of watery whey and seven loaves were my diet from that cleric and
    seven years I lived upon that food.

'In this place did my dark curragh seek its rest; from embarkation till then
    was my seven years' exile.

'Seven more years passed, and then a salmon was my portion, brought to
    me by a shapely otter, a deed of heavenly mercy.

'Said I, "No uncooked salmon shall I eat, please God; my compliments to
    Him, but throw it back!"

'At that, the same otter brought me back a noble unscathed fish, while
   another brought me firewood.

'Like a man, the industrious brown one crooked his paw and blew me up a
   fire.

'Seven years more did I live so, with blameless merit; the course was clear,
   each day brought evidence of God's promise in an edible gift.

'After seven years, and fasting for three days, my kind and powerful King
   and Apportioner sends me half a loaf and a morsel of fish.

'The filling of my crystal cup is also a great marvel; each night it dispenses
   health-giving essence to sustain me.

*'Neither cold, nor heat, nor tempest, nor biting wind disturbs me here, by
   the ever-victorious power of the kingly King.'

†Our famous companions remained with him, receiving food the like of his
   — a feast arranged in likeness of the Fianna.

Each man received his cupful, each had his half-loaf and morsel of fish — a
   fine arrangement!

The ancient prophesied: 'You will find your own land safely; though you
   meet your foes, you will not kill them.'

33 ISLAND OF THE FALCON

Then they found an island full of flocks, a good harbouring, a successful
   exploit; here they found a falcon of Ireland.

They rowed after, following it swiftly, hastening over the waves to their
   enemies' island.

---

* The clemency of the weather in the Otherworld has often been remarked upon, from the *Odyssey* through to Arthurian traditions of
the Isle of Avalon.
† The Fianna were the troops led by Fionn MacCumaill (Finn MacCool). Their provisioning and billeting arrangements were ordered
fairly, so that every man ate alike. This put paid to the feuds that might break out if one man was given a better portion than another.
King Arthur's Round Table is founded upon a similar, equatable principle.

His foes made peace with brave Maelduin, in the sight of each warrior;
after sureties and pledging, they returned to their own land, a
prosperous voyage.

Many strange things, many wonders, many mysteries made up their story,
as swift Maelduin tells them.

Long life and peace stand with me in this rich world; may I enjoy glad
company by the grace of the kingly King.

At my death, may I travel to heaven beyond the fierce and violent host, till
I reach the Angels' Kingdom, the high place of notable company.

*The wondrous voyage of Maelduin shows forth the mysteries of heaven's
glory; the generous poet, Aed Finn, sun of Ireland's wisdom, recited it.

†Ten times twenty is the numbering of this sacred song, it has no small
power; sing seven verses before it, then read ten; this is the noblest
recitation.

* We are told that the *immram* reflects the mysterious voyage to heaven. Aed Finn was the poet who arranged and recited these verses.
† Here we find the magical power of the poem. Celtic stories and poems often end with a charm or blessing. The manner of the charm here directs the reader to chant seven prayers of empowerment first and then to read ten verses of the poem for best effect. Unfortunately, this prayer-formula does not survive in modern Celtic tradition. It is possible that the reader may have used it to invoke the seven angels assigned to the days of the week. (See C. Matthews, *The Elements of Celtic Tradition*.)

Retelling and Commentary

The following retelling of the prose edition of the *Voyage of Maelduin* is accompanied throughout by a commentary, set in smaller type and in two columns.

Maelduin was the son of a warrior, Ailill Ochair Agha, and of an abbess of Kildare, raped by Ailill while on one of his youthful raiding adventures. After his return from this raid, but before the birth of his son, Ailill was killed by raiders from Laighis. The abbess called her child Maelduin or 'Bald One'; as it is shameful for a nun to have a child, she sent him to be fostered by the Queen of the Eoghanacht of Ninuss and raised as her own son, along with her three boys. Maelduin grew strong and handsome, outstripping his fellows in every game. One day, after he had been victorious as usual, one of his peers, a proud young warrior, taunted Maelduin with his lack of parentage. Much bemused, since he understood himself to the child of the King and Queen, Maelduin went to the Queen, and swore that he would neither eat nor drink till she told him the truth.

The Queen brought him to the abbess, his mother. Maelduin begged to be told who his father was. She said that he would not be gladdened by this news, since Ailill had been dead long since. Maelduin returned to his father's kindred and was welcomed among them. One day, he was idly casting stones in the graveyard of a church when Briccne, one of the monks, harangued Maelduin: 'It would be better to avenge the one lying there than cast stones over his bones.' Then Maelduin learned of his father's murder at the hands of raiders from Laighis. Intent on vengeance, he discovered that the best way to approach his enemies would be by sea. Accordingly, he consulted the druid Nuca, who instructed him in the building of a magical curragh or skin-boat. It was started on an auspicious day and put under druidic charms. Nuca told him to sail with only seventeen companions to attack his enemies. Maelduin chose his special friends, German and Diurán, to be among these. They were about to embark on the most auspicious day when Maelduin's three foster-brothers swam out to join the crew. Although Maelduin bade them return, he could not see his brothers drown. But the additional numbers caused the adventure to go awry.

They sailed to the raiders' island and heard them drunkenly boasting of past triumphs, including the murder of Ailill. German and Diurán rejoiced too soon that their thirst for vengeance was to be quenched, for the wind blew the boat away from shore and they became lost at sea. Seeing their boat aimlessly drifting, Maelduin bade the crew rest their oars and trust to God. He blamed his foster-brothers for their untimely appearance.

Maelduin's conception follows a common Celtic pattern: he is conceived irregularly, the posthumous offspring of a warrior with a nun for a mother. Celtic heroes tend to have one mortal and one otherworldly parent, or one secular and one holy parent, as in this case. Conceived between night and morning by a nun and a layman, Maelduin therefore has a predisposition to excel in both the everyday realms and the mysterious Otherworld, and is destined to sail between them with facility. The taunting of Maelduin for his lack of parentage is an important feature of the story, since it brings him face to face with a different reality and the necessity of growing up. For a youth who thought himself of royal stock to be suddenly told that his parentage is unknown would have been a profound shock in such a traditional and status-conscious society as ancient Ireland.

The story mingles pagan and Christian themes very skilfully. Maelduin, in seeking vengeance for his father, goes automatically to a druid for counsel. It is the wise Nuca who directs the building and launching of the curragh in which they make their *immram*. He also instructs Maelduin to sail with seventeen men who, with Maelduin, make eighteen or twice nine. Nine was a number that the Celts considered most fortunate. The otherworldly islands to which they sail are rooted in the potent pre-Christian culture of Ireland, even though some appear to be colonized by monks and hermits. The exploration of inner states of being is not the preserve of any one religion: the Celtic Otherworld is open to all.

Maelduin's voyage moves from the world where men and deeds of arms predominate into the Otherworld, where women and wonders abound. The dangers he encounters do not always require a warrior's skill or courage, but rather instinct, caution and mother wit. This *immram* becomes a profound initiation for Maelduin, enabling him to enter into mature adulthood. His motivation for embarking is vengeance on his father's murderers; his *immram* virtually becomes an education conducted by his absent father from the other side of death, putting us in mind of Aeneas' descent into the underworld to consult his dead father in Virgil's *Aeneid*.

But what begins as a vengeance quest ends as an exploration of the Celtic Otherworld; by the end of the voyage, vengeance has become irrelevant when set beside the wonders and terrors of the *immram*. In this, the *Voyage of Maelduin* parallels the Grail legends. *Peredur*, one of the earliest manifestations of the Grail story, begins as a vengeance quest; the later medieval *Quest del Saint Graal* ends as the attainment of transcendent illumination of spirit.

The character of Maelduin is daring and mature; he is carefully responsible for his men, controlling their wilder urges, while never reserving himself from danger. He may also be considered a touch weak-willed when it comes to ladies and potent berries. His companions, German and Diurán, complement him well: German is forthright and argumentative, while Diurán is curious and canny. This well-matched threesome may be contrasted with the three enthusiastic but unfortunate foster-brothers who cause the *immram* to take place by their ill-advised appearance.

ISLAND OF GIANT ANTS

They sailed for three days and nights until they heard the crash of waves upon land. Turning to the north-east, they found an island whereon dwelled swarms of giant ants, the size of foals. These tried to devour the crew and their boat. The men fled.

The onset of the voyage provides a period of reflection when the men are alone with the elements. Their fears are represented by the giant ants, the first of many such encounters with enlarged animals and beings. This facility of telescoping size is a common feature in shamanic travel to the Otherworld. Lewis Carroll's *Alice in Wonderland* is a prime example of this tendency. The initial experience of the inner traveller is often one of fearful anticipation. Travelling in the Otherworld often brings up underlying anxieties and self-doubts, especially when confronted by the unknown. All spiritual voyaging is undertaken alone at the beginning. Greater experience lends confidence, but loneliness is the initial stumbling block, bringing up the question, 'Who am I in actuality?'

ISLAND OF MANY BIRDS

They came next to an island with many terraces, on which numerous birds perched. Maelduin himself went on to the island and brought back many birds to eat.

The men begin their quest for food, which sometimes becomes an overwhelming urgency. The Otherworld provides an abundance of good things, though there are often conditions which have to be observed if the men are not to transgress the bounds of hospitality. Birds are animals of otherworldly speech, often appearing as messengers. Here they provide Maelduin with the means of staying alive in this strange environment. It is important to take appropriate nourishment so that we may better attune to and receive the gifts of the Otherworld.

ISLAND OF THE HOUND-FOOTED HORSE

The next island they found had upon it a horse with hound's legs. With the eagerness of a dog, it leaped at them in order to eat them. When it saw them flee, the strange animal dug up earth and stones to throw at them.

This is the first of three islands – the others being 4 and 8 – where horse-like creatures behave in a bizarre way. The horse was a prime animal of reverence in Celtic tradition. Such a combination of the eagerness of a dog, the speed of a horse and the dexterity of a human being is nightmarish. This is one of many encounters in which the men themselves are a potential part of the food-chain: a salutary experience for those who are used to being the aggressors. Our first explorations on the inner journey are often confused, rather like the jumbled dreams which succeed a busy day. With time we learn how the Otherworld fits together.

———— ISLAND OF INVISIBLE RIDERS ————

German drew the lot to explore the next island, but Diurán accompanied him. They found enormous hoof-prints, each one the size of a sail, in the sand, and the debris of great feasting. Made fearful by the size of what they saw, both men returned speedily to the ship from which they were able to view a horse-race and hear the sound of riders encouraging their steeds, but no riders could they see.

The crew receive their first intimation that they are not the only intelligent species in this realm. At this point, none of them has the sensitivity to see the otherworldly beings who live here, though they hear voices. This corresponds to the manner in which inner voyagers begin to comprehend the extent and organization of the Otherworld, a chastening experience.

———— ISLAND OF PLENTEOUS SALMON ————

A whole week of near starvation brought them to an island where a house stood on the sea-shore. One door faced the sea; it had a stone valve that opened when the plenteous salmon carried by the water struck it, allowing the fish to tumble into the middle of the house. The house was unoccupied but there was a bed set ready for Maelduin and a single bed for every three of the crew, not to mention food and drink of the richest sort. They fell upon the food and praised God.

This island and number 24 show the totemic power of the salmon, one of the most important otherworldly animals in Celtic tradition, associated with great memory, inspiration and abundance. The otherworldly hostel set ready for the crew is a reflection of the hospitality that was offered to travellers in ancient Ireland, where inns and hostels were governed by special laws. Hospitality is still a sacred duty among many indigenous peoples today. Here the men experience the abundance and open-handedness of the Otherworld, which is rich in nourishment to those seared by the hard commercialism of our own world.

ISLAND OF TREES

They came to an island of trees. Maelduin took a branch from one of them as they passed it; after three days, three apples began to grow on it which sustained them for forty days.

In Celtic tradition, the apple is a fruit of eternal life, in contradistinction to the fruit of the paradisal tree in Eden. To their diet of birds and fish is added fruit. The wondrous apple bough is a scion of the otherworldly tree of tradition that nourishes the spirit. (The Edenic fruit of the Tree of Good and Evil is not called an apple, though it is conventionally symbolized in this way.) The island, they discover, is like the paradisal realm of the British Otherworld, Avalon, the Island of Apples, where King Arthur is said to have been restored to health. On this island the travellers learn to let their gifts and perceptions mature, an important aspect of shamanic journeying.

ISLAND OF THE REVOLVING BEAST

The next island had a great beast upon it which moved swifter than thought. It turned itself round and round and inside out, never at rest. It no sooner achieved one form when it shapeshifted into another. It threw stones at the ship when it saw the crew escaping, one piercing Maelduin's shield and lodging in the boat's keel.

One of the main features of shamanic journeying is the manner in which the shaman can shapeshift from human to animal form. In order to become a shaman at all, the candidate must suffer a wound or illness that makes this ability possible, so it is significant that Maelduin's shield and the ship are pierced at this island. This is an important part of the voyage, for it enables changes to begin.

ISLAND OF CANNIBAL HORSES

They then discovered an island of great horses, the sight of which delighted the eye of any lover of horseflesh. However, each horse attacked the other, tearing and eating each other until blood poured out everywhere.

The sight of horses attacking and eating each other is probably one of the more horrific sights to any Irishman, used to the universal Celtic reverence for the horse. Even today, in Britain and Ireland, horseflesh is not eaten by human beings. The horse is therefore one of the prime totemic animals, whose flesh is taboo. The senseless slaughter of beautiful animals on this otherworldly island reflects the way in which humans prey on each other in the world. Only by such a shocking vision are we shown the futility of warring on each other.

ISLAND OF FIERY PIGS

They sailed away swiftly, in low spirits, not knowing where they would find land or help. They arrived at the next island in sad shape, hungry, thirsty and depressed. When Maelduin and his men landed, they found the ground hot, heated by the fiery pigs who slept in caverns underground. There were trees with golden apples upon them. Red pigs struck at the apple trees so that the fruit fell and so they could eat from dawn till sunset. During the hours of darkness, they slept. From dawn till twilight, many birds swam around the island, landing at twilight to eat the apples. The men gathered apples to sustain them and were glad of the small respite from hunger and exposure to the sea.

At their lowest ebb, the voyagers see a wondrous sight of both otherworldly birds and underworld pigs eating the apples here. The men share this food, though they cannot live in such a fiery environment. In shamanic and folk tradition, humans are often helped by animals when they are in great need. Pigs are the animals of the underworld, the place of ancestral wisdom in Celtic tradition. In British lore, Merlin learns from the pigs during his madness in the Caledonian forest. Here the voyagers learn that beings of all species and worlds can live together in harmony.

ISLAND OF THE CAT

Nearly dead from hunger and thirst, and sickened of the sea, they came to an island with a lime-whitened fortress upon it. Inside the wall of lime was one of chalk, and the tower almost touched the clouds. They entered the largest house within the enclosure and found a cat leaping from pillar to pillar. A splendid feast was laid ready and around the room were great treasures, stacked in rows. Maelduin asked the cat if the food had been left for them. He felt that it had been, so they set to. One of Maelduin's foster-brothers coveted a necklace and asked if he could take it. Maelduin forbade him, but the foster-brother disobeyed, concealing it about his person. As he reached the middle of the enclosure, the cat leaped through him like a fiery arrow and burned him to ashes. Maelduin returned the necklace, cleansed the ashes from the floor and scattered them over the sea.

The seemingly cosy guardian of the treasures on this island turns out to be quite the reverse, and the first of the extra men is lost here. This island teaches the travellers that the laws of their own world also apply here, although much is strange to them. Inner journeying may tempt us to relinquish our common sense, but it is a good passport to travel under nevertheless. Respect and good manners are just as important in the inner realms.

————ISLAND OF BLACK AND WHITE————

They came to an island divided by a brass fence. On one side of the fence was a black flock of sheep; a white flock was on the other. When the shepherd who guarded them threw a black sheep into the other half it turned white; when he threw over a white sheep, it turned black. Maelduin determined to test this effect by throwing a peeled white wand into the black portion so that it turned black. They returned to the boat, still weary and hungry from this adventure.

This island represents a deeper level of experience for the voyager. It features many times in Celtic tradition and marks one of the primary borders of this world with the Otherworld. The reversal of black for white and vice versa is at first confusing, but it shows the Otherworld's ability to reveal the opposite of any situation, feeling or action. The one who governs this experience is the shepherd, a threshold guardian who often challenges those who enter the Otherworld. He shows the traveller that confidence hides a kernel of fear and that fear hides a kernel of courage.

————ISLAND OF GIANT CATTLE————

The third day following, they found an island of pigs, captured one and ate it. German and Diurán went to explore further. They found a wide, shallow river but when German dipped his spear into it, it burst into flames as though the water had been fire. They could see giant cattle protected by a herdsman on the other side of the river. German beat the remains of his spear-shaft upon his shield to frighten the cattle. 'Why are you frightening the calves?' cried the herdsman. 'Where are the mothers of these calves?' asked German, amazed that cattle larger than those before him could exist. 'They bide over the mountain,'

THE VOYAGE OF MAELDUIN

replied the herdsman. German and Diurán returned to the ship and, on Maelduin's advice, the crew rowed wearily away.

Another herdsman appears on this island, showing the voyagers that there are certain boundaries it is wise not to cross. Over-confidence and bravado are worthless in the Otherworld; only exact skills and ruthless self-knowledge will serve here.

────ISLAND OF THE MILL────

The next island had a mill and a surly old miller. The crew inquired about the mill and were told that it was called the mill of Innbir the Senant. Apparently, half the corn from Ireland was ground there; it came from those people who begrudged each other or acted in an ungenerous way. They saw the countless loads and the burdened people arriving and hurrying away, signing themselves against the mill.

Although the Celtic Otherworld is not a place of judgement, the deeds committed in life carry their own reward. The mill or turning tower is a common feature of Celtic stories, symbolizing a place of torment or burden where our natural dispositions are refined. Anciently, all grain was ground by the local miller, an unpopular figure who often took more than his own share. A period of service within the mill is often required, depending on the individual concerned. A heart burdened or obscured by grudges cannot range throughout the freedom of the Otherworld and must be cleansed at this point. The experience of this island resonates well with number 32. (See C. Matthews, *Arthur and the Sovereignty of Britain*.)

────ISLAND OF SORROW────

They came to an island of black-clad and lamenting people. One of Maelduin's foster-brothers drew the lot to go there; he too became a mourner as soon as he landed. Maelduin sent two men to rescue him, but they also fell to wailing. Then four men were sent to rescue these two; Maelduin bade them neither to look at the ground or the air, nor to breathe save through their cloaks. These four men were successful, delivering the two that had gone before them from the island. The foster-brother, however, was left behind. On their return, when asked why they wept, the two men said 'We did as we saw others do.'

This island represents the state into which inner travellers fall when they refuse the challenge of island 13: they fall into lamentation of the past, its unfairness, and the restrictions it places upon present actions.

While a period of mourning or moaning is healthy, this is not a place at which to stay forever. All living beings must suffer loss and feel the pain of grief, but there are other islands to explore. The second foster-brother, however, remains on the Island of Sorrow.

ISLAND OF THE FOUR FENCES

The next island had four fences dividing it into four enclosures: a golden one with kings inside; a silver one with queens inside; a brass one with warriors inside; and a crystal one with maidens inside. A maiden brought hospitality, serving them from a little vessel. They lay drunken for three days, and woke on the third day within the body of their own boat.

Here, the crew are greeted for the first time by an otherworldly maiden. Subsequent encounters, on islands 16, 23 and 27, reinforce the importance of women in the inner world. The Otherworld is the natural domain of women, in which they act as guardians and initiators. The everyday world is the natural province of men, in which they are active and dominant. Like islands 11 and 12, this one challenges the travellers to find their correct place or vocation. The otherworldly food offered by the maiden is too strong for their present capabilities.

ISLAND OF THE CRYSTAL KEEP

They came to an island where a crystal keep and bridge were found. The bridge could not be crossed and would throw men backwards. A woman emerged from the keep with a pail in her hands and lifted a crystal slab to draw up water. German demanded a welcome for Maelduin but was rebuffed. Before the door of the keep was a brass net with musical blades which, when shaken, made the men sleep. On each of the following three days, the maiden came out again and rebuffed them. Lastly, she welcomed each by name and gave hospitality. Her great beauty impressed them. Her prophetic foreknowledge had told her of their coming. She took them into her house and served each man with food and drink. The crew tried to persuade her to sleep with Maelduin but she said she was unsure and would give her answer on the morrow. The next day, they found themselves in their ship once more.

The perilous or narrow bridge is a feature of the Otherworld. Only the truly dedicated can cross it. The boorishness of the crew in insisting that the hospitable woman sleep with Maelduin shows their unreadiness to enter the Otherworld proper. Their attempted abuse of hospitality is punished when they are sent back summarily to their boat. The tests of islands 10, 11, 12, 15 and 16 are those of recognizing boundaries and understanding the nature of otherworldly and earthly exchange. On this, the voyagers' second proper encounter with a being of power, they fail in courtesy and preparedness.

ISLAND OF SINGING BIRDS

Towards the north-east they heard the harmony of great chanting as though a choir were singing the Psalms. As they neared the mountainous island they saw that the song was that of birds.

Druidic tradition speaks of the 'perpetual choirs of song', the choirs of bards whose retelling of the ancient, traditional songs and stories wove together the mundane and inner worlds. This tradition was partially transmitted to the Celtic Church whose monks, like those in the rest of the Christian world, chanted the Psalter (the 150 Psalms of King David) every day. The ancient Celtic and pre-Celtic lore, however, was and continues to be maintained in the Otherworld. The harmony of this perpetual song is heard by the travellers to this island, which marks the mid-way point of their *immram*. Birds are often the bearers of otherworldly tidings. This island denotes the place where we listen to the voice of the Otherworld.

ISLAND OF THE ANCESTORS

They found a small island with many trees upon it. Here a hermit lived, clothed only in his hair. He had left Ireland on pilgrimage and had been shipwrecked. He saved himself by placing a sod of Irish turf under him from which the island was formed, which continued to grow for ever more. Each year another foot and another tree was added to it. The birds in the trees were the souls of the hermit's ancestors awaiting judgement, and they were fed by angels. A half-loaf of bread and a piece of fish was the ration of every being on that island, with water from the well to sustain them. The hermit prophesied that all but one of Maelduin's crew should reach home.

This is the first of four islands (the others being 19, 29 and 32) on which the voyagers meet a hermit. The Irish missionary Church recognized three forms of martyrdom: red martyrdom was death at the hands of an opponent of Christianity; green martyrdom meant severe penance; and white martyrdom was exile in a foreign land. The monks of the Celtic Church often achieved white martyrdom as they were responsible for the conversion and civilization of much of north-west Europe. Some, more adventurous than others, chose to live as hermits on islands off the western seaboard of Ireland. One such notable location was Skellig Rock, an inhospitable and barren island off the coast of west Cork. The Island of the Ancestors brings knowledge of the ancestral realms. It is formed by the faith of the hermit who trusts in his native earth, and so it becomes a place where pilgrims learn about the element of earth itself. This is the first of four islands which teach the gifts and challenges of the elements, the others being 20, 21 and 22. Here Maelduin and his crew are given reassurance of their return, all save the last foster-brother who, at this point, is still with them.

ISLAND OF THE HERMIT

On the third day following, they found an island surrounded by a golden wall. A hermit lived here sustained by a well of nourishment that yielded water and whey on Fridays and Wednesdays, milk on Sundays and feast-days, and ale and wine on other feast-days. They each drank their fill and slept from afternoon to morning. After three days, the hermit asked them to leave and so they set out.

The food well which generously gives forth on this island is equatable with the well of plenty belonging to the Goddess of Sovereignty in Celtic tradition. In many stories concerning the making of kings, we read of an encounter with the Goddess wherein she offers different beverages – milk, wine, ale, whey etc. – depending on the virtue and status of the individual who meets her. Each liquid conveys a distinct gift as well as nourishment. According to the Celtic Church, each day of the Christian calendar was accorded a different status: solemn feast-days of Our Lord or Our Lady – such as Christmas or Candlemas – merited special foods; while the feast-days of saints, apostles and martyrs merited somewhat better food than the ferial or ordinary days. This island teaches the travellers about appropriate forms of nourishment and challenges our views on abundance and scarcity. The Otherworld usually provides an abundance of whatever is scarce within the mundane realm; this is one reason why so many people travel in the inner worlds. There is also a reciprocal exchange, for the mundane world has an abundance of whatever the Otherworld lacks. There is an important ecological balance to be maintained between the worlds.

ISLAND OF THE FORGE

Ahead they saw an island from where they heard the hammering of smiths. The following conversation came on the breeze: 'Are they near?' 'Who's coming?' 'Those little boys floating in their trough.' Maelduin ordered the men not to turn the boat but to start rowing backwards. With the stern foremost, they began their retreat. The voice came again, 'Have they landed yet?' 'They are neither coming nor going.' 'So what are they doing now?' 'They are further away than before.' Then the giant smith came from the forge and lobbed a lump of red-hot iron at them which made the sea boil.

Smiths were held in awe in Celtic society, for they had the alchemical secret of crafting metals, regarded to be a magical activity. The ancient skill of smelting ores from the earth into implements is now paralleled by the chemical processing of uranium – a natural deposit in the earth – into nuclear power. The uses and abuses of such power, which may be used for peaceful as well as aggressive purposes, point to the importance of impeccable responsibility and dedication to the skills of smithcraft. This island represents the discovery that the human achievements of any one generation are puny compared with the eternal and archetypal works of the Otherworld. It also teaches the gifts and challenges of the element of fire.

SEA OF GLASS

At last, the sea turned clear as crystal, so that the sea-bottom could be seen clearly. They spent a day sailing across its magnificent surface.

This next encounter marks a transitional stage in the voyage. Between this sea and the Pillar of the Silver Net (number 25), Maelduin and company are prepared for the last stage of the journey. The clear sea is like the clarification of the soul that is accomplished after considerable hard work and spiritual effort. In the *Voyage of St Brendan*, St Brendan's crew are terrified of this sea because it reveals to them all the possibilities they had never thought of. The Sea of Glass represents the gifts and challenges of the element of water.

SEA OF MIST

The sea changed and became cloudy, giving the crew the sense that it would not support the ship. Beneath the waters they saw forts and countryside. A monster in a tree attempted to eat the herd of cattle a warrior was guarding. It seized an ox and devoured it while the warrior ran away. Maelduin and his crew grew terrified, for they felt that their fragile boat would pass through the waters as through mist.

The next sea becomes like mist and seems, to the travellers' perception, to be unable to support them. This sea symbolizes the difficult stage of trusting the process of the inner journey when there is no prior experience with which to equate it. The Sea of Mist represents the gifts and challenges of the element of air.

ISLAND OF RECOGNITION

They came to an island surrounded by cliffs. When the people of that place saw them coming they screamed, 'It is they,' in great panic. A large woman came forward and pelted them with hazel-nuts, which they collected. The people seemed relieved when the crew returned to the ship, for it was apparent that there may have been a prophecy concerning travellers that might come and conquer the island.

This island is strategically placed at the very gates of the deepest Otherworld enclosure. The inhabitants represent those who have undergone a certain amount of experience or who have made a partial *immram*. They feel threatened by those who aim to complete the journey. The islanders, perhaps unwittingly, gift Maelduin's company with hazel-nuts, the Celtic fruit of knowledge, thus equipping them for the next stage of the journey.

ISLAND OF THE RAINBOW STREAM

The next island had a rainbow stream which went up over the island, flowing onto the opposite strand. Within this stream swam salmon which the voyagers could catch as they fell upon the island in vast heaps. The air was thick with their odour and it was impossible to gather them all up. From vespers on Saturday to prime on Monday the stream was motionless. The crew gathered up plenteous quantities of fish and continued searching the seas.

This island presents one of the most beautiful visions of the whole *immram*. Like island 5, abundant salmon can be found here; but the rainbow stream denotes an even greater wonder, for it represents the gifts of the Otherworld which flow unendingly and are always available. The juxtaposition of the salmon of this island and the hazel-nuts of the preceding one is significant, for the travellers have all the otherworldly sustenance they will need for the last stage of the voyage.

PILLAR OF THE SILVER NET

They rowed till they found a four-sided pillar of great height in the middle of the sea, with not a sod of earth around it. From its summit hung a silver net through which the boat passed. Diurán struck it with his spear. 'Do not destroy the net,' cried Maelduin, 'It is the wondrous work of great ones.' 'I take some in God's name,' said Diurán, 'that our story may be believed in Ireland. I shall offer it to the altar of Armagh if ever we return home.' Two-and-a-half ounces of that net remain in Armagh. From the height of the pillar they heard a great voice uttering, but they did not speak its language.

The Pillar represents a significant gateway on the *immram*, for it shows the way into the deepest realms of the Otherworld. The travellers have seen many wondrous things, but they have never been exposed to such a mighty creation as the pillar. On the shamanic journey, passing beyond the net or veil signifies a deepening of experience, a greater confidence and trust, although it does not mean that there are not still tests in store. We note that from this point onwards the terrors that surround the inmost circle of the Otherworld cease. The voice that they hear is almost certainly that of Manannan mac Lír, God of the Otherworld.

————————ISLAND OF THE SHUTTERED DOOR————————

The next island stood high above them on a pedestal. Although they rowed about it, no approach could be found, only a locked door at its foot. Above they could see a plough, but saw no-one to speak with.

Just as island 23 represented incomplete knowledge of the Otherworld, so this island represents the potentiality of knowledge accessible within it. The travellers are unable to penetrate this first island of the inmost circle which seems to act very much as a guardian of the Otherworldly gates.

————————ISLAND OF WOMEN————————

They came to a large island with a massive interior plain covered with grass. A great fortress stood near the sea, a beautifully appointed house with soft beds. Seventeen nubile maidens were preparing a bath. As the crew landed and made their way to the fort's entrance, Maelduin remarked, 'That bath is being prepared for us.' They saw a richly dressed horsewoman coming towards them, who entered the fort. One of the maidens came and said, 'The Queen welcomes you, enter here.' Maelduin sat with the Queen and his men with each of the maidens while they feasted. The Queen bade each man take the maiden next to him and retire to the canopied cubicles where the beds waited, while Maelduin slept with the Queen. They slept till dawn. The Queen said, 'Remain with us and you will not grow older. You shall have immortality and enjoy what you enjoyed last night. Be no longer wanderers of the wave.' When Maelduin asked how she came there, she replied, 'I was married to the King of this island to whom I bore these seventeen girls. He died and left no successor, so I ruled in his place and everyday I go out to judge the community and guide its affairs.' 'Why do you need to leave us today?' Maelduin asked. 'Because, unless I judge the people, you will not enjoy the delights you had last night.'

They stayed for the three winter months and it seemed more like three years. The crew grew restless and wanted to return home. 'We shall never find the like of this at home,' said Maelduin. 'Stay here and enjoy your woman, then, but we are going home,' they said. Maelduin reluctantly accompanied them but, as they left, the Queen threw a sticky clew of thread at Maelduin and drew him back. They stayed thrice three months and resolved once more to leave. 'If the thread strikes Maelduin, we will be brought back to this place,' they said. 'Then let some other catch it,' said Maelduin. Again they embarked and the Queen threw her sticky thread. One of the crew caught the ball and his hand was severed by Diurán, so that they might escape. At that, the Queen began to wail and cry, and that was how they escaped.

This is one of the most famous islands of all the *immrama* stories. The tradition of an island whereon a group of women or priestesses guard the earthly paradise is told in Celtic stories and medieval legends alike. One such place is Avalon, where Morgen and her eight sisters reign. It is significant that Maelduin's arrival at the Island of Women is his twenty-seventh disembarkation: twenty-seven is a multiple of the sacred number nine; his crew should have been eighteen, another multiple of nine. Maelduin is unable or unwilling to leave here due to the fact that he has had his sexual initiation, becoming the consort of the Queen of the Island of Women. She is an aspect of the great Goddess of the Otherworld whose reflection we can still discern in the Faery Queen of folk tradition. Maelduin's union with her brings him a deeper fulfilment than he has known before. This island brings immediate fulfilment of desire and refreshment of spirit; it also teaches lessons about life's purpose. Here time does not run and the seasons are constant. This cessation of cyclic time can only be borne by those who are immortal, however; the absence of the turning seasons becomes disorientating for mortalkind and they are compelled to travel onward.

ISLAND OF BERRIES

They were driven by the waves to an island where many-fruited trees grew. Berries of great size grew upon them; and the task of tasting them fell upon Maelduin. He squeezed some juice into a cup and, after drinking from it, fell into a sleep for twenty-four hours, totally senseless, so that it was unclear whether he was alive or dead. When he awoke, Maelduin bade the men gather more berries, for they were good. The crew mixed them with water to lessen their effect and rowed away.

This island provides a cleansing forgetfulness that heals Maelduin of his desire to return to the last island.

Many travellers make the otherworldly journey to seek healing of one kind or another; the Island of Berries and the remaining islands provide different forms of healing or cleansing that help the traveller realign his or her energies physically, mentally, psychically and

spiritually. This island brings restoration to the essential inner self and is experienced, to some degree, each night in dreams which connect us to the inner realities.

ISLAND OF THE EAGLE

They landed on a large island with a lake. There was a small church where a grey hermit lived, clothed in nothing but his own hair. He said that he was one of Brendan of Birr's company who had gone on pilgrimage. All had died save he. He showed them Brendan's stone, which they had brought with them, and the men bowed before it in reverence. The hermit bade them eat sparingly of the sheep, and so there they stayed for a season.

One day, while exploring the island, they saw a great, ancient eagle which alighted near the lake. It carried the branch of a tree from which red berries like grapes depended. The men hid and watched and, under Maelduin's direction, took some of the berries for themselves. In the afternoon they saw two younger eagles, who tended the old bird and stripped its feathers of lice. They crushed the berries and threw some into the lake to make it red and the ancient eagle bathed therein. The young birds continued to groom the eagle until, on the third day, it rose restored to strength and with fresh plumage. Diurán also bathed and drank of the waters, so that thereafter he remained forever youthful, losing neither hair nor tooth to age. They bade farewell to the hermit, provisioned the boat with sheep and set off once more.

This island brings the experience of complete renewal. The ancient eagle is restored to full vigour and is able to fly away as strong as any young bird. Diurán shares in the healing bounty of the berry-reddened lake and proclaims his experience to all people he meets thereafter by the amazing youthfulness of his form. It is

often remarked that those who engage in spiritual pursuits remain miraculously youthful in appearance. This is part of the otherworldly exchange: those who uphold the harmony of the inner realms are themselves upheld by otherworldly powers in the mundane realm.

ISLAND OF JOY

Many people filled with laughter dwelled upon the next island. The lot to explore fell on the third foster-brother who immediately joined the inhabitants in laughing and playing, as though he had known them all his life. The crew left him there.

THE CELTIC BOOK OF THE DEAD

This is the reverse of island 14 and is, in some respects, the ante-chamber to island 31. The foster-brother who is left here enters into the most joyful state he is able to attain, and the crew is once more back at the appointed druidic number of eighteen. Like the other voyagers, he does not enter island 31 which is reserved for those who have committed their mortality into the keeping of the Otherworld. This island brings the fulfilment of island 27 but without remembrance of the mundane world. It is a place of festival and of glad rejoicing because it connects us with the healing grace of shared companionship.

──────ISLAND OF CIRCLED FIRE──────

They came to a small island, circled with a fiery, revolving wall. When the doorway to the fortress faced them, they saw beautiful people feasting and enjoying themselves. They heard the music and delighted at the marvellous sight, but were unable to enter.

This is the innermost island of the *immram*, wherein the fullness of the Otherworld is found. It is guarded by a ring of fire and revolves so that no-one can enter it unaware. That fire is the white fire of the *sidhe*, the faery place of peace, which burns away mortality. The most archetypal ideas, forms and patterns are within this island, and all those who are within rejoice in their creation and preservation. They are guarded well in this the inmost centre, but we must not imagine them as only remaining here: concepts and archetypes ripple out from this island to be filtered down into our own world. Some share of them is found in the other islands of the *immram*, but their full richness is experienced here. As Maelduin and his men retain their human condition, they are unable to attain the full experience of this island. The happy Otherworld this island represents is portrayed in many Celtic stories, and is properly the abode of the Lordly Ones, the Faery Folk or otherworldly beings.

────── ISLAND OF OTTERS ──────

Not long after, they found a white island shaped like a bird, on which there was a man clad in his own hair making prostrations on a rock. They asked his blessing and demanded to know who he was. He had been the cook of a monastery on Tory Island. He was an ex-thief who used to steal from the church and garner away all his ill-gotten spoils. One day, when he attempted to dig the grave of a sinful man over a holy one, he was frightened by the holy man's ghostly voice. It promised him hell if he persisted in his enterprise, but heaven if he stopped. The cook demanded to know how this could be proved in advance. His answer came when the grave began to fill by itself.

After that, the cook went to sea with his treasures. Strong winds took his boat and he became aware of a ghostly holy man beside him. The ghost instructed him to cast away his ill-gotten goods into the sea, and the cook obeyed. Eventually, he landed on a barren rock and was miraculously fed by otters who brought him salmon. By their providence, he wanted for nothing. The otters brought similar provisions for Maelduin's men. Before they left, the cook prophesied that Maelduin would reach his destination and find his father's killer, but that he should forgive him.

The cook's voyage, rather like that of Maelduin, is initiated by selfish intentions. From acquisitiveness and greed, the cook is brought to a place of scarcity where he learns to appreciate the simple things once again. We are shown that the most unregenerate person can make an *immram* and discover the inmost self, but only by throwing overboard the luggage that encumbers his or her journeying. This island brings freedom of spirit to the inner traveller and marks the way back home.

ISLAND OF THE FALCON

They came to an island whereon much livestock grazed. Suddenly, they saw an Irish falcon which guided them south-eastwards towards Ireland. They found a small island very like the raiders' island, upon which they had been about to land when they were blown off course. The crew listened at the door of the fortress there and heard those within discuss what they should do if Maelduin came. Maelduin accordingly knocked on the door and was given welcome. They went within and were welcomed, and they related all their adventures.

All journey's ends are marked by a symbol or landmark that brings connection with our home; for the travellers, an Irish falcon appears, giving them new hope. After the many fantastic beasts of the Otherworld it is great relief to see a familiar bird. This island represents the return to everyday reality, a place where the traveller can become earthed in the mundane world. This is a crucial feature of inner journeying that is frequently overlooked. Unless we are grounded and re-established in our own time and place, we are likely to become fey, accident-prone and adrift from our life's purpose. It is therefore important to mark the journey's end by humanizing actions, as Maelduin does, by eating, meeting other human beings and reporting his *immram* to them. Maelduin forgives his enemies and relates his adventures to them, so that the gifts of the inner journey are immediately shared.

the Many-Coloured Land

Do not fall on a bed of sloth,
Let not thy intoxication overcome thee,
Begin a voyage across the clear sea,
If perchance thou mayst reach the land of women.

Voyage of Bran mac Febal

In *The Celtic Book of the Dead*, I have assigned each of the islands visited by Maelduin to a card that depicts a scene from each island. These cards may be used for taking your own *immram* and methods for this are given in Chapter Four. Each of the *immram* cards is depicted on the following pages, together with the Celtic background to the experience of each island, its divinatory meaning and a challenge for the querent (the person consulting the card) to address. In addition there are two Guide Cards, representing the *anam-chara* or soul friends of the voyager who show us the otherworldly wonders. Separate from the *immram* cards are the Gift Cards, each of which represents an empowering aspect of the Otherworld.

Island of Giant Ants

BACKGROUND
When we first set out upon the *immram*, the wide expanse of the sea is around us like a great void and we are beset by fears. This island presents us with the challenge of facing our worst fears realized. Insects become terrible when they are large as beasts; similarly, our worst fears are not normally looked at too closely for fear of their implications.

MEANING
Your worst fears realized. A complete petrification of effective action. Niggling worries. Attention to detail. Industrious action. Co-operation.

CHALLENGE
Look closely at your fears and analyse what they are based upon. You will be shown the strengths and weaknesses they obscure. By facing fear you partially overcome it.

 I

IMAGE

A series of giant ants threatens the small curragh.

Island of Many Birds

BACKGROUND
The abundant birds of this island are like the many possibilities that surround us in life. In the middle of such abundance it is easy to become confused.

MEANING
Discontent. You are spoilt for choice. Indecision. Starving amid plenty. Inability to concentrate. Trying to do too many things. The need to assess your gifts. Abundance.

CHALLENGE
Start to appreciate the riches and resources that lie about you in your life. If you cannot decide upon a course of action unaided, then assign one of the Gift Cards to each option and let the gods decide (*See* pages 94–97).

 2

IMAGE

A high cliff full of sea-birds.

Island of the Hound-footed Horse

BACKGROUND
When domestic animals turn against humans, the natural order seems threatened.

MEANING
Confusion. Best friends turn upon you. Certainties prove unstable, positions and prospects mutable. Hypocritical friendship. Rejection.

CHALLENGE
Be more sensitive to those about you. It is possible that you are putting burdens and responsibilities upon others that you might better carry yourself. Are you upholding or betraying friendship?

3

IMAGE

A hound-footed horse threatens the voyagers.

Island of Invisible Riders

BACKGROUND
Maelduin's men hear the contending shouts of invisible riders, all boasting that their horse is the best. In a world of conflicting opinions, it is often difficult to find the right motivation, but the fruits of unrealized concepts may never ripen without true purpose.

MEANING
Trying too hard. Being overwhelmed with speculations. Lack of belief in oneself. Living off past glories. Empty words. Dreams that will never be fulfilled. Self-delusion.

CHALLENGE
Are you making a mountain out of a molehill or are you afraid to let your ideas grow and manifest? Believe in yourself and do not be swayed by the opinions of others.

 4

IMAGE
Otherworldly horses canter across a beach heaped with treasures.

Island of Plenteous Salmon

BACKGROUND
The sustenance of the Otherworld nourishes Maelduin's company when they most need it. When we are in deepest need, the remedy often lies close to hand.

MEANING
Rest. Respite. Recovery from struggle. Rightful reward or recompense for efforts. A period of reflection. Generosity without strings.

CHALLENGE
Are you too satisfied with your present way of life? Are you unable to relax? Allow yourself a respite when the going gets tough.

 5

IMAGE

Salmon fall into the interior of a welcoming otherworldly house.

Island of Trees

BACKGROUND
In Celtic tradition the apple is always a fruit of immortality, healing or fulfilled desire, unlike the apple of the Judaeo–Christian Fall which betokens sinfulness. The branch of apples from which Maelduin eats is from the ever-living tree of the Blessed Islands, which assuages both hunger and thirst.

MEANING
The ability to savour the natural gifts of life. Gratitude. Awareness of natural rhythms. Patience.

CHALLENGE
Are you content with the little things of life? Be careful that your desire to possess does not become obsessive.

 6

IMAGE

Maelduin holds an apple bough from which three apples grow.

Island of the Revolving Beast

BACKGROUND
Many Celtic characters undergo a physical contortion or agitation when excited or grieved, including the famous hero Cu Chulainn, whose exertions become so violent he has to be doused in a cauldron of cold water. The magical ability to shapeshift is attested in many stories.

MEANING
Mental contortion. Stress. Showing off.

Trickery or illusion. Changeable nature. Failure to recognize the true state of things. Vulnerability.

CHALLENGE
In your current position, are you trying to stretch your abilities to match the situation or the situation to match your abilities? Something is not working because you have not allowed for its basic nature. Give everything its due.

 7

IMAGE

A fantastic beast which undergoes many transformations.

Island of Cannibal Horses

BACKGROUND
Here animals act like human beings and start attacking each other. In Celtic tradition, the horse is the supreme animal of power and strength, making this image doubly threatening.

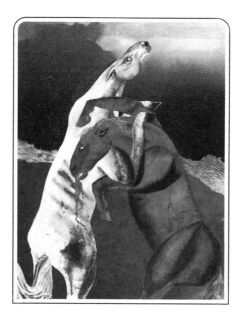

MEANING
Misuse of power. Jumping to conclusions. Inability to react honestly. Rage. Aggression. Violent thoughts.

CHALLENGE
Do you need to be aggressive? Resort to arbitration if you can. Get your facts straight: consult the horse's mouth first! Negotiate or haggle.

 8

IMAGE

Wild horses battle.

Island of Fiery Pigs

BACKGROUND
In Celtic tradition, pigs are animals of the Underworld, and the gift of the ancestral world to our own. Birds are normally messengers of the Otherworld. Here, both sets of animals eat of the trees in an orderly fashion. The two worlds are shown to be in harmony with each other.

MEANING
Timeliness or *kairos* (the appropriate time).

Being in the right place at the right time. Expectation of news. Renewal. Realization of goals. Adequate provision of needs. Harmonious partnership. Ecological balance.

CHALLENGE
If you find it hard to achieve your desire, do not envy others. Are you using the abilities of others to achieve what you want? Try to work harmoniously with others.

 9

IMAGE

On the left of the apple tree, we see pigs searching for apples by daylight. On the right of the tree, fantastic birds come to perch in its branches by starlight.

Island of the Cat

BACKGROUND
The rules of otherworldly hospitality entail respect for people and property found therein. Because we may be in unusual situations does not mean that we can act discourteously.

MEANING
Caution is needed. Respect. Stasis. Entrapment. Restlessness and dissatisfaction.

Impulsiveness. Theft. Appropriation of other's things or resources. Honour. Integrity.

CHALLENGE
Have you violated the rules of society by your actions? Your thoughtless actions affect others and sometimes hurt them. Find out what the boundaries are in this situation and abide by them.

 IO

IMAGE

We see four pillars connected by chains, and a multiplicity of treasures, while the cat leaps between pillars.

Island of Black and White

BACKGROUND
In the Otherworld, everyday reality is reflected by its opposite as though in a mirror. Where black becomes white and white becomes black, it is difficult to know just where we are. The only person who can regulate this change is the shepherd who knows the reality and powers of both worlds.

MEANING
Reversal of good fortune to bad luck or

bad luck to good fortune. A shock. Startling change. A chance to appreciate the mutability and natural rhythm of life. Challenges to deeply held beliefs.

CHALLENGE
Are you clear about what you intend and the changes it will bring? Only by appreciating your current position can you judge. Look at the opposite side of the argument.

I I

IMAGE

A landscape divided by a fence with sheep on either side; the shepherd heaves one across.

Island of Giant Cattle

BACKGROUND
In Celtic tradition, the giant herdsman of cattle is a well-known guardian of thresholds. Often surly and unhelpful, he will give advice and warning.

MEANING
Biting off more than you can chew. Provocation given or received. The goal is before you but you are prevented from attainment. Over-confidence.

CHALLENGE
There will always be some things that defeat you, however hard you try. The inability to trust those who may know better could be preventing you from reaching the right decision. Concentrate on learning more about yourself. Perfect your skills.

12

IMAGE

Beyond a fiery river, we see a herdsman watching grazing cattle.

Island of the Mill

BACKGROUND
The otherworldly mill is where the spectres of our greed are fed to us. What we desire binds us with unbreakable links so we are enslaved to it.

MEANING
Niggardliness. Possessiveness. Scandalmongering. Anger and jealousy. Selfishness. Co-dependency. Grudges and feuds.

CHALLENGE
What are you holding on to that is unnecessary in your life? Let the gift of generosity come into your heart. Let other people live without your control. Lift burdens from others' backs.

 I 3

IMAGE

People bearing sacks on their backs approach a mill.

Island of Sorrow

BACKGROUND
Many Gaelic stories juxtapose regions of happiness and sorrow, which are not seen as positive or negative conditions. Irish musicians would play three kinds of music: the sleep-strain to bring dreams, the joy-strain to bring happiness and the sorrow-strain to bring tears. All three are necessary for a balanced existence.

MEANING
Primal misery or angst. Sorrow. The gift of tears. Mourning. Inability to express sorrow. Sharing of pain with others. Loss.

CHALLENGE
Social convention bids us hide away pain and sorrow. It is permissible to mourn. Do not allow yourself to get out of touch with your feelings. Are you living in the past?

 **14**

IMAGE

A pillar-stone on which is an image of extreme grief, with a woman lamenting.

Island of the Four Fences

BACKGROUND
This island shows the four estates of humanity: gold represents material desires, silver represents artistic attainment, brass indicates strength of arms and crystal betokens spiritual attainment. The food of maidens from the crystal enclosure is too strong for the crew.

MEANING
Inappropriate behaviour. Failure to recognize where you should be or which direction you should take. Vocation.

CHALLENGE
Are you envious of other people's attainments and their possessions? Discover your own specializations and needs. Are you in the right job or situation?

 **15**

IMAGE

An island divided by four enclosures. A king holds a rod of power, a queen holds a cup, a maiden a looking-glass, a warrior a spear.

Island of the Crystal Keep

BACKGROUND
Here Maelduin's company have a prevision of the Island of Women, but their lack of preparedness betrays them. In many stories, otherworldly people vanish as soon as they are asked their name or to reveal a secret. Here German asks to know the secret of the island.
His answer is a forgetful sleep and the vanishing of the island.

MEANING
Confused motivation. The inappropriate use of one thing for another. Insensitivity. Lack of preparedness. Pomposity. Seeking to run before you can walk.

CHALLENGE
Are you appropriating the work, concepts or things of others? Weigh up your desires against the known facts. Are you properly prepared? Listen to your dreams.

16

IMAGE

On a narrow bridge stands a maiden hauling up a bucket.

Island of Singing Birds

BACKGROUND
Birds are often the guardians or messengers of the Otherworld. In British Celtic tradition, the birds of Rhiannon grant vision of the Otherworld and bring healing or forgetfulness to those in pain or sorrow, as do the birds of Clíodna in Irish tradition.

MEANING
Sensitivity. Ease of heartache. News. The voice of intuition or conscience.

CHALLENGE
Are you listening carefully to the sub-text of what is being said by others? Listen to the messages your body and heart are telling you.

 **17**

IMAGE

A sea-girt island around which birds wheel, singing.

Island of the Ancestors

BACKGROUND
This island exemplifies reverence for the ancestral earth of our homeland. This card represents the challenge of the element of earth.

MEANING
Slow expansion by steady work. A little at a time. Ancestral strengths and abilities. Love of home. The need to be rooted in one activity or place.

CHALLENGE
By steady work and trust, your boundaries can be increased. Make sure you conserve your energies sensibly. Work at what you do the best. Reliance on traditional frameworks gives you strength that cannot be shaken. Where is your spiritual foundation or belonging?

 18

IMAGE

A turf-like island upon which a hermit sits by a well.

Island of the Hermit

BACKGROUND
Fridays and Wednesdays are days of fasting and abstinence in Christian tradition.

MEANING
Sufficient resources. An ability to get by on the minimum necessary for life. The daily round of life. Spiritual reserves. Self-control.

CHALLENGE
Are you getting the nourishment appropriate to your needs – not only food, but also cultural and spiritual nourishment? Do you have a continual feeling of either scarcity or abundance? Seek out and maintain a balanced diet that will sustain your whole being.

 19

IMAGE

A hermit shows the miraculous streams of liquor that nourish his solitude.

Island of the Forge

BACKGROUND
The smith was one of the most respected craftsmen in Celtic tradition, one whose ability was virtually magical. This island represents the challenge of the element of fire.

MEANING
Daring in the face of danger. Swift action. the ability to conserve resources when the going gets rough. Lack of caution. Enthusiasm. Creativity.

CHALLENGE
Do you know when to pull in your horns? There is no virtue in staying to fight when flight is more appropriate. Run away to fight again another day. Does your life lack warmth?

 20

IMAGE

An enraged smith waves his hammer at Maelduin's boat.

Sea of Glass

BACKGROUND
This sea represents the challenge of the element of water.

MEANING
Ability to assess and discern clearly. Perception. Psychic skills. Vision. Clarification will come.

CHALLENGE
If the clarity of every situation is perceptible to you, you may find a very critical streak within you. Learn to assess without judging. Is love lacking in your life?

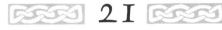 **21**

IMAGE

A clear sea wherein fish are swimming.

Sea of Mist

BACKGROUND
This sea represents the challenge of the element of air.

MEANING
Disorientation. Obscurity. Difficulty in assessing things clearly. Mental confusion. A temporary loss of direction. Putting trust in the unseen. Insubstantiality.

CHALLENGE
At times of instability we must learn to trust the constants of our life, for they give us support. Find your strengths when you are strong and they will help you when you are disorientated. What needs liberating in your life?

 **22**

IMAGE

Looking as it were into the sea's depths, we see a serpentine monster with a cow in its jaws. The herdsman retreats.

Island of Recognition

BACKGROUND
On this island, Maelduin's company are repelled by people who are fearful of something or someone else. We note that they do not wield real weapons, but nuts – the Celtic symbols of wisdom. The people here are like those who are on the verge of enlightenment: they keep others at bay but are fearful of proceeding further themselves.

MEANING
Needless fears. Foolish doubts. The need to be recognized or acclaimed. Memory. Incomplete knowledge. Misunderstanding. Fear of what people say.

CHALLENGE
Trust your instincts or gut-reaction to a situation and you will not be let down. Is there something in your life you are avoiding coming to terms with? Are you fearful of letting go?

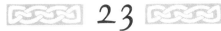 **23**

IMAGE
A woman throws a handful of nuts towards the boat.

Island of the Rainbow Stream

BACKGROUND
Primal abundance and promise are betokened on this island, where Maelduin and his men see more fish than they can carry back to the boat. The salmon is the fish of wisdom, knowledge and omniscience in Celtic tradition.

MEANING
Abundance. Harmony. Beauty. The accomplishment of a project. Reward for hard work. A shower of good fortune.

CHALLENGE
Look for beauty in the heart of everyone, and seek to live harmoniously with all species. Otherworldly gifts are yours with practice.

 24

IMAGE

Salmon fall in a mighty stream along a rainbow-like arch of water.

Pillar of the Silver Net

BACKGROUND
This pillar marks the boundary of the far regions of the Otherworld. Once they sail beneath and through it, Maelduin and company are beyond the realms of everyday reality.

MEANING
New possibilities arising. Imagination. Creation. Trust. The will of God/dess. Letting go.

CHALLENGE
Are you daring enough to pass the boundaries of your daily life and go exploring in the realms within? If you unloose your imagination you may find new currents on your life's journey that will lead you to where you most desire to be.

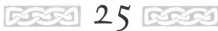

25

IMAGE

Through the meshes of a silver net, we see the calm sea stretching ahead. A mighty pillar reaches to the sky.

Island of the Shuttered Door

BACKGROUND
In nearly every *immram* there is one impenetrable place or veiled secret. The plough at the top of the island represents the ability to work constructively and fruitfully.

MEANING
Hidden knowledge. Secrets. Abilities unacknowledged. Potentialities.

CHALLENGE
Only you can unlock the door to your inmost self and abilities. Do not treat your abilities as treasures too precious to use.

 26

IMAGE

A high island upon a pillar with no approach to it, save a locked door at its foot. A plough can be seen above, but no living person.

Island of Women

BACKGROUND

The Island of Women represents the earthly paradise wherein Maelduin's company are warmly welcome. To remain here means never to return to reality, however. To be immortal means relinquishing the human condition.

MEANING

Inspiration. Enchantment. One's beloved or heart's desire. Homesickness. Contentment. Divine

discontent. Desire fulfilled. Discovering your life's purpose.

CHALLENGE

When the need to experience everything has been assuaged, even the heart's desire wanes palely. In what direction do you most need to grow in order to learn? What do you need to relinquish to be a real human being? Do not allow the links of desire to bind you.

27

IMAGE

The Queen of the Island of Women holds a cup in welcome. Beyond lies a house of gold thatched with white birds' feathers.

Island of Berries

BACKGROUND
After the enchantment of the Island of Women, Maelduin seeks a needful forgetfulness.

MEANING
The need to return to reality. Forgetfulness. Healing sleep. Satisfaction. Transition. Coming to your senses. Welcome relief from illness or trauma. Convalescence.

CHALLENGE
After the excitement of success or the disruption of problems or illness, the return to the daily round needs to be prefaced by a period of transition. Pick up the old rhythms gently. Is your addiction to substances or habits unbalancing your life?

 28

IMAGE

Maelduin lies in a drunken stupor beneath the berry-bearing tree.

Island of the Eagle

BACKGROUND
The eagle is one of the most respected birds of Celtic tradition, endlessly renewing its life and having a long memory.

MEANING
Transformation. Memory. Refreshment. Holiday or needed change of circumstance. Time to change your life positively. Renewal.

CHALLENGE
Do you go on till you drop from exhaustion? Are you tired of life because you never refresh yourself? Take a break. Allow new influences to come into your life.

29

IMAGE

An eagle emerges from a reddish lake, wings spread in triumph.

Island of Joy

BACKGROUND
The Island of Joy is twin to the Island of Sorrow encountered earlier.

MEANING
Primal happiness. Remembrance of past friends or places. Enjoyment. Rejoicing. Festival. Celebration. Gladness. Companionship.

CHALLENGE
Our society imposes the strict duty of enjoyment, but rarely gives us access to the freedom of deep happiness. Such moments are rare, so open your heart to the things that make you feel joyful.

 **30**

IMAGE

A stone pillar-head with a ritualized mask of joy. Around it, people rejoice and dance for joy.

Island of Circled Fire

BACKGROUND
In most *immrama*, the sailors cannot enter or pass a certain place. Here, the picture is one of otherworldly perfection. Because Maelduin and his men have chosen not to stay in the Island of Women, they choose mortality and cannot enter where immortals feast in joy.

MEANING
Self-sacrifice. Joy in another's pleasure.

Giving. Compassion. Better prospects ahead.

CHALLENGE
To see with the eyes of others is a great gift. The Otherworld gives us the ability to empathize and learn compassion, gifts that must be used in our own world. This view of better conditions may seem unattainable now; what is preventing you from crossing the threshold of that attainment?

 3 I

IMAGE

The picture is ringed with fire. Beyond we see otherworldly beings feasting and playing.

Island of Otters

BACKGROUND
Here Maelduin finds the guide for his return journey home. While he was buoyed up with hatred and vengeance of his father's killers, he could not remain in Ireland. Now he forgives them and is ready to go home. The otter or water-dog is one of the most important spiritual totems of animal-guides in Celtic tradition.

MEANING
Forgiveness. All situations turn out well. A free heart. The ability to share. Peace. Adaptation. Freedom. Simplicity.

CHALLENGE
Whatever preys upon our mind will never let us rest until we face it and allow it to change. There is no such thing as unalterable good or evil, only resolution and adaptation. Forgive and forget.

 **32**

IMAGE

Otters bring gifts of fish, fire, fresh water and a wheaten loaf.

Island of the Falcon

BACKGROUND
Again, one of the totem birds of the Otherworld appears, this time to guide them homeward.

MEANING
Welcome. Return. Conclusion. Homecoming. Resolution. Objective perception. The assimilation of life's lessons.

CHALLENGE
The ability to read the signs of the times and to act upon them is the mark of an experienced traveller in the realms of mortality. The landmarks of your home are also those of your spiritual home.

 33

IMAGE

In the rays of the setting sun, a falcon swoops over a curragh. The land of home shows on the horizon.

The Ever-living Lady

She is the archetypal Woman of the Blessed Islands. She comes to many visionaries and dreamers to invite them to the Otherworld, but does not reappear until the voyagers reach the Land of Women. She is the inspirer of those who need to travel into the depths of the inner worlds.

BACKGROUND
The earliest *immram*, the *Voyage of Bran mac Febal*, is initiated by the visit of an otherworldly woman who encourages Bran to make an *immram* to the Island of Women. Although she is nameless in this tale, she is from the shores of Tír nan Beo, the Everliving Realms where travellers are refreshed.

MEANING
She invites us to leave behind the everyday world and to travel within to find the realization that we seek. She represents the need to relinquish our own will and to be open to the winds of change that blow from other shores.

IMAGE

An otherworldly woman of great beauty, who holds in her hands a crystal globe.

Barinthus

He is the pilot and guide of many *immrama*, including that of St Brendan's voyage. He is a hardy master-mariner who has undergone many voyages and now acts as a ferryman between the worlds of everyday reality and the Lands of the Living. He is the pilot of the homeward voyage from the enlightenment of the Otherworld to the realm of the everyday world.

BACKGROUND
Geoffrey of Monmouth's *Vita Merlini* tells how the poet Taliesin and the seer Merlin took the wounded King Arthur to Avalon after the Battle of Camlan. They were guided thither by 'Barinthus to whom the waters and the stars of heaven were well known'. St Brendan the Navigator also consulted with Barinthus about his *immram* to find the Land of Promise.

MEANING
Barinthus acts as the pilot who leads voyagers back home after their *immram*. He helps us work towards manifesting our otherworldly dreams.

IMAGE

A mariner of mature years, with his hand on the oar of a curragh.

The Apple

IMAGE
An apple from the otherworldly tree.

BACKGROUND
Unlike the apple of the Judaeo–Christian Fall or the classical apple of discord, the Celtic apple is symbolic of the earthly paradise, of wholeness and healing.

MEANING
Desire fulfilled. Wholeness. Healing.

CHALLENGE
What is your heart's desire? Eliminate the 'oughts' and 'shoulds' from your heart.

The Silver Branch

IMAGE
A rod-like branch, from which hang nine round, silver bells.

BACKGROUND
The silver branch was borne by Irish master-poets in token of the great otherworldly tree which was always in flower, fruit and blossom simultaneously.

MEANING
Forgetting or remembering. Otherworldly communion. Inspiration.

CHALLENGE
Take the mastery of your accomplishments in both hands and become effective in your own realm of influence.

The Hazel-nut

IMAGE
A hazel-nut held in the mouth of a salmon.

BACKGROUND
The Well of Segais, in the Boyne Valley, was the mystical source of knowledge. Poets sought to eat of the salmon who ate the nuts that fell from the nine hazel-trees there.

MEANING
Wisdom. Counsel. Inspiration.

CHALLENGE
Test the situation facing you now with your senses. How does it look at first glance? What feedback do you hear? How does it feel to you? Does it accord with your taste? What is your gut reaction?

The Wheel

IMAGE
An eight-spoked wheel.

BACKGROUND
The wheel is a common symbol in Celtic mythology. It is often used to depict the sun. Arianrhod, the British Lady of the Silver Wheel, is the mistress of destiny.

MEANING
Change. A new cycle. Destiny fulfilled or changed.

CHALLENGE
How can you use what you have learned in the past to good advantage now? What recurrent features can you discern in your life?

The Green and Burning Tree

IMAGE
One half of a tree is shown in leaf, while the other half of the foliage is aflame.

BACKGROUND
This is one of the primal images of the Otherworld in British Celtic tradition. To encounter it signifies the change from one mode of being to another.

MEANING
Choice. Your voyage is not yet finished.

CHALLENGE
If you do not like the outcome, change it by free choice.

⟡

The Dragon-stone

IMAGE
A ruby-red crystal globe is grasped in the bird-like claw of a dragon.

BACKGROUND
The dragon-stone was considered to be a symbol of great strength and to possess invincible qualities.

MEANING
Adamantine strength will overcome all difficulties.

CHALLENGE
The ability to succeed in your intent lies within your hands. Act resolutely, with the courage of your convictions.

The Four-sided Cup of Truth

IMAGE
A four-sided vessel.

BACKGROUND
The four-sided cup of truth belonged to Manannan mac Lír, and was given, by him, to Cormac mac Airt. If three lies were said over it, it would shatter in pieces; but if three truths were said over it, it would reunite.

MEANING
Judgement. Truth. Discernment.

CHALLENGE
Are you supporting some person, thing or habit at great cost to your own integrity? Do not be so intent upon the broken fragments of your life that you prevent it from becoming whole again.

◇

CHAPTER FOUR

the Game of Life

A noble pastime: men and women together,
Playing pleasant games without competition,
Under the bright boughs
Without blame or guilt.

Voyage of Bran mac Febal

The *Immram* Deck is intended to be a companion and guide through the shoals of life. It can be consulted at crisis points when reflection, caution and counsel are needed. At these times, we usually lack the necessary objectivity to perceive our situation. By asking the cards and plotting the pattern of *our* voyage according to the nine realms or stages of the journey shown on the reading cloth, we begin to discover the answers that have been lying within us, waiting to be discovered all the time.

Although not predictive like the tarot, the *Immram* Deck *is* a method of divination. The true definition of divination is 'a method of asking the Gods'. The cards depict the thirty-three otherworldly destinations of Maelduin's voyage, the two guides upon the *immram* and the seven otherworldly gifts that travellers receive, thus offering divinatory gateways to clearer perception. The challenges encountered on the islands reflect the full gamut of life's experiences from a different perspective.

Two reading methods are given in this chapter: *Immram* One and Two. Both of the *Immram* methods take us on a journey. As we know, the experience of travelling away from home gives us fresh insights and modes of perception; similarly, the experience of returning home brings us new insights about our environment and our place within it.

In this chapter we explore ways of using the *Immram* Deck, the kinds of journeys we can take with it and methods of interpretation, as well as addressing some queries and issues surrounding its use.

IMMRAMA READING METHOD

The general instructions that follow are for *Immram* One or Two. More detailed instructions are given later in this chapter.

Step 1. Draw from choice, or sight unseen, your pilot on the *immram*. If you draw the Ever-living Lady, you start your journey at Harbour and voyage to Landfall: the Lady represents the journey *into* the self. You will be taking *Immram* One, the Outward Passage. If you draw Barinthus, you start your journey at Landfall and voyage to Harbour: Barinthus represents the journey *from* the depths of the self *to* self-awareness in the real world. If you draw this card, you may already have been on an *immram* that is drawing to its conclusion. You will be taking *Immram* Two, the Homeward Passage. On the reading cloth provided, place your Guide Card in the top left-hand position as marked.

Step 2. Take and shuffle the *immram* pack, making sure that the cards are all upright, pondering all the while on your question/problem to resolve etc. When you feel that you have 'put' your question or problem into the pack, cut the cards in your preferred way and start laying them out. Place one card face down on each of the nine realms in the order drawn. Turn them over and interpret each card with the aid of the book, allowing the picture's face-value and images to dictate the meaning or feeling of the reading, as well as the written meaning and the significance of the card being placed on a particular realm. This is the *immram* or spiritual voyage you will take to seek clarification or confirmation.

Step 3. The next procedure is optional. At the conclusion of an indecisive reading, you may need to draw one of the Gift Cards, which represent a gift from the Otherworld. One is drawn to clarify the course of action required. This is placed on the Gift position at the top of the cloth.

CHOOSING A GUIDE

When we are about to set off into unknown regions or undertake a task in which we are unskilled, we seek a suitable guide who is both wise and experienced. Taking an *immram* is no exception.

Some of us travel in search of answers; some of us have realized the answers but are unsure about their implementation. The two *immrama* suggested here can be applied to either condition. The Outward Passage may represent an ongoing journey which leads us to see fresh possibilities and new openings. The Homeward Passage is often one of return to responsibility or commitment where the fresh insights of the *immram* can be practically utilized.

In life, there is no such thing as a journey without end. The fictional ongoing voyages of the Starship Enterprise in *Star Trek* are just that – continually ongoing, never returning home to reassess, rest and live normally. Few real people have that stamina and commitment: most of us need respites and the opportunity to return to the comfortable and mundane world of home.

The Guide Cards provide two different ways of taking your *immram*. The Ever-living Lady is an immortal, otherworldly woman. She helps us discover the inner realms which are her dwelling place. She initiates us into the realm between the celestial and marine worlds which border her world. All that lies between is unknown to us: we recognize neither the functions nor the implications for us of this realm. We go as open-eyed and sometimes fearful children into its wonders. She guides us, but it is our curiosity and resolve that keep us on course.

Barinthus is a mortal man who has the facility of a walker between the worlds. He helps us to return to the realms of mortality and not to become entangled with the complex wonders we have witnessed. He has travelled these waters many times as a pilot; he knows the best courses to plot and the welcome we are likely to receive upon each island.

He initiates us back into our mortality, for the *immram* has taught us maturity and patience. He guides us home, but it is our desire to live effective lives that keeps us on course.

There are times when we need a different voyage or just a glimpse of a map. When you are unsure which *immram* you need to take, ask each of the guides to direct you. Take both Guide Cards from the pack and contemplate first one, then the other. One or other should give you a definite feeling of 'yes' or 'no'. If you are uncertain of how to read your own reactions, then contemplate each Guide Card and draw one *immram* card at random. This one card may give you a glimpse at the map of your voyage and a certainty of which guide is best for you at this time. When you are reading for others you can use this same method to help make a decision.

Travel broadens the mind and presents us with new possibilities on return. Those who will not change do not grow; such folk seldom journey anywhere in case they are stretched beyond the narrow frameworks they are accustomed to inhabit. If you do not want to change, then do not take an *immram*. On the other hand, do not rush into voyaging before you count the cost: Maelduin's foster-brothers joined the voyage at the last moment and were all left behind. One succumbed to greed, one to sorrow and the other to joy. In fact, they each received the reward of their own nature; this is one of the basic laws of the Celtic Otherworld, which is based on justice, inspiration and wisdom.

IMMRAM ONE: THE OUTWARD PASSAGE

The reading cloth has nine positions arranged as a voyage or journey. The illustration *opposite* shows the realms numbered ready for you to take *Immram* One, the Outward Passage. Choose this *immram* when you are seeking an answer to a problem or situation and use the Ever-living Lady as your guide.

THE MEANINGS OF THE REALMS

1. Harbour: where you are now.

The Harbour represents your present position or standpoint. At the beginning of any journey it is good to take stock and assess your resources. In Tsarist Russia, it used to be customary for the intending traveller to sit down ritually before setting out, in order to appreciate the home and place of establishment. Read the card in this realm lovingly and savour its full worth.

2. Realm of Many Colours: source of your dissatisfaction, worry or problem. The reason why you have started this voyage.

The Realm of Many Colours represents the urge to travel. Many journeys begin as quests, although they can also be escapes. Whatever the circumstances surrounding your *immram*, whatever excuses you make to yourself, the card in this realm represents the springboard from which you make your journey. It will often show the underlying difficulty which has acted like the grit that makes the oyster's pearl.

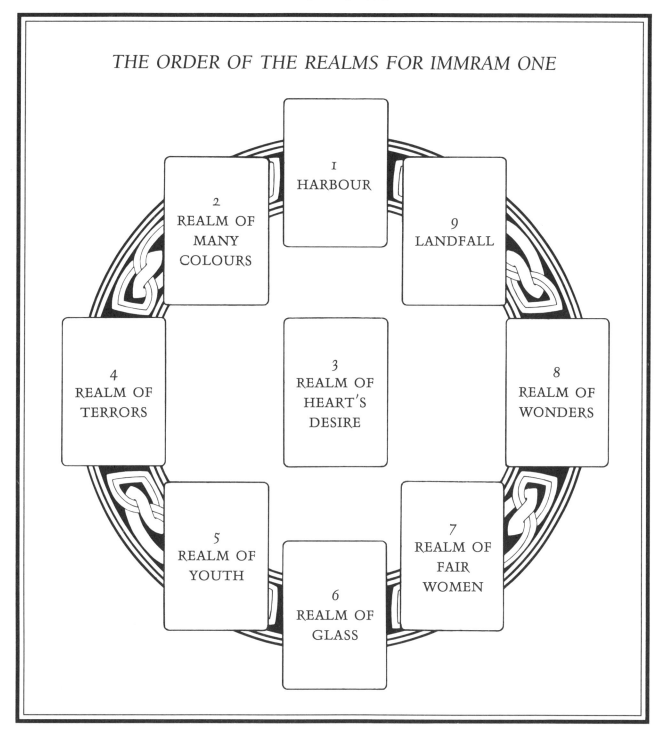

THE ORDER OF THE REALMS FOR IMMRAM ONE

1 HARBOUR

2 REALM OF MANY COLOURS

9 LANDFALL

4 REALM OF TERRORS

3 REALM OF HEART'S DESIRE

8 REALM OF WONDERS

5 REALM OF YOUTH

6 REALM OF GLASS

7 REALM OF FAIR WOMEN

3. **Realm of Heart's Desire: what you seek; your ideal solution, vision-quest or dream.**

The Realm of Heart's Desire lies at the heart of the reading as the aim of your quest. Many of us day-dream fruitlessly, while others hardly dare dream about their heart's desire. Sometimes we are so skilful at suppressing what we deeply desire that we have to meditate long to realize it. The vision-quest is a dedicated setting-aside of time and energies in order to discover the heart of desire: this sometimes involves a going-forth into the wilderness where the ancestral and spiritual helpers may speak in clear visions or dreams. Read the card in this realm carefully, for what you truly desire you will achieve!

4. **Realm of Terrors: your fears and uncertainties; things that hold you back.**

The Realm of Terrors represents that stage in the journey when its intrinsic difficulties begin to be overwhelming. This is often a time of turning back, of not feeling adequate or suitably prepared. These fears might be assuaged if the traveller went forward boldly, improvising and facing each challenge as it happens. An *immram* is a voyage that stretches our potential. Meeting the unknown is often terrifying because there are neither rules of engagement nor prior preparation. Read the card in this realm objectively, and begin to overcome the terrors by familiarizing yourself with the terrain.

5. **Realm of Youth: your strengths; skills, abilities and talents that help you.**

The Realm of Youth represents the part of the traveller that is confident and able. It is usually the card that shows us the best means of journeying or of overcoming difficulties. The natural abilities that we each possess are seldom utilized to their fullest extent, but are wasted. The card in this realm asks you, what talent of your own lies untapped or neglected that would help you now?

6. **Realm of Glass: who or what hinders you.**

The Realm of Glass represents the people and circumstances that prevent you from voyaging with a good heart. These may be duties and responsibilities, a lack of time to assess your position or else these may be friends, family or opponents. The Realm of Glass tends to contort our perceptions and intensify problems like a burning-glass. It is extraordinary how many hindrances begin to litter our way when we first attempt to walk a spiritual path. Read the card in this realm perceptively but without judging or condemning anyone.

7. **Realm of Fair Women: who or what helps you.**

The Realm of Fair Women represents the people and circumstances that help you in your voyaging. They may be people who give you encouragement and a space to moan or exult. Or they may be circumstances in which you flourish and feel strong. These support networks in your life are necessary, and you should not be too proud to lean upon them when the going gets tough. Read the card in this realm expansively and generously and bask in its meaning.

8. **Realm of Wonders: otherworldly or ancestral gifts that aid you; hidden factors yet to manifest.**

The Realm of Wonders represents the part of the voyage that cannot be predicted. We tend to wrap our lives up, pin them down and tabulate them, so that we know where we are going. There is never any telling when you are going to be washed up in the Realm of Wonders. Any random wind or change of current could bring you here and your life could change utterly as a result. Here you see into the sacred dimensions of the gods; here you remember the delights of childhood; here you access the deep memories of your ancestors. Treat the card in this realm as a free surprise gift whose use you may have yet to discover.

9. Landfall: how you resolve your problem or question.

Landfall represents the last island before your voyage home and the return to mundane affairs. Here lies buried the map that will help you make that return. Your course of action, or lack of it, will be determined by your careful reading of this map. Your homeland is in sight. Read the card in this realm with resolution and see what capacity for change or acceptance lies within you.

IMMRAM TWO: THE HOMEWARD PASSAGE

Barinthus is your guide for *Immram* Two. To take *Immram* Two, reverse the course of *Immram* One, and voyage from Landfall to Harbour. Choose this *immram* when you have a good notion of the circumstances surrounding the problem or situation, but feel uncertain about how to proceed. With Barinthus as your guide, you are making a return home in full awareness of what your *immram* has shown to you. You have been to the heart of the otherworldly islands; therefore the emphasis of your return will be somewhat different than the journey outwards.

THE MEANINGS OF THE REALMS

1. Landfall: the way back home. What is your best course of action?

Landfall represents the first glimpse of solid ground after a long voyage. How will you resolve your problem? The reality of return lies before you and challenges you to find the best course. Plot your course, allowing for the tides and currents of your own nature.

2. Realm of Wonders: ancestral memory, communion with the divine. What is the source of holiness and wholeness in your life?

The Realm of Wonders brings us remembrance of the deep places. It is to such sources that we go in order to drink and be refreshed for our daily life. Bring this gift back with you and be aware of how the whole of life is connected. There are many possibilities and new wonders that may emerge in your everyday life if you keep this memory fresh.

3. Realm of Fair Women: needs and inadequacies. What is the source of love in your life?

The Realm of Fair Women gives you the love of friends and family, and of times and places that spur you on. The card in this realm encourages you to draw upon that loving help when you most need it. Identifying and expressing need is something we can only do in the company of those with whom we feel comfortable. Joy, truth and wisdom enhance the gift of this card for you.

4. Realm of Glass: deceptions and difficulties. What is the source of anxiety in your life?

The Realm of Glass has no power to deceive one who has sailed to the verges of the Otherworld. You see the distortions for what they are: magnifications of circumstances and fears that once threatened to overwhelm you. Deep at the heart of this realm is a mirror into which you look for guidance when blockages and difficulties arise. The mirror now shows you the card in this realm. Sift its meaning for you and bear it as a personal shield which will reflect problems back on themselves.

THE ORDER OF THE REALMS FOR IMMRAM TWO

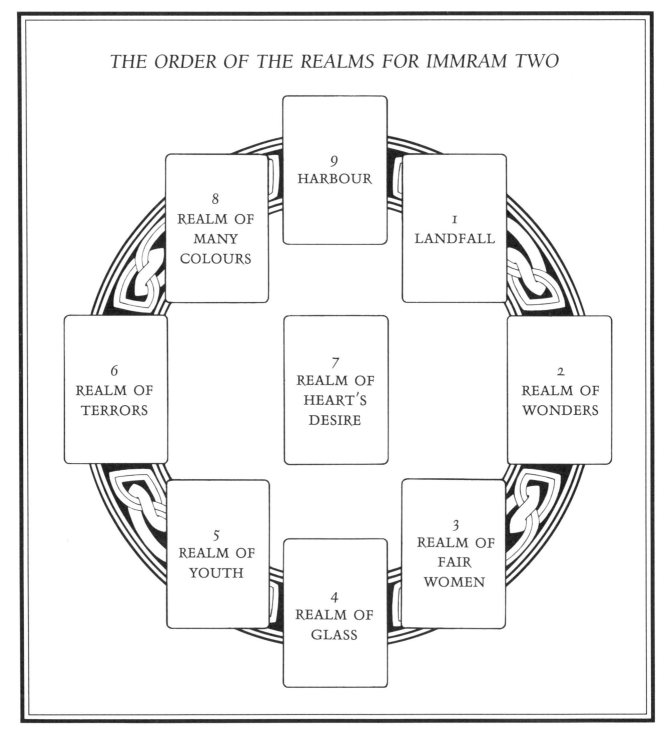

9
HARBOUR

8
REALM OF
MANY
COLOURS

1
LANDFALL

6
REALM OF
TERRORS

7
REALM OF
HEART'S
DESIRE

2
REALM OF
WONDERS

5
REALM OF
YOUTH

4
REALM OF
GLASS

3
REALM OF
FAIR
WOMEN

5. Realm of Youth: recreation and renewal. What is the source of creativity in your life?

The Realm of Youth has restored your strengths and abilities. It shows you new ways in which you can maintain your talents and learn new skills. This becomes a realm of recreation and play for your spirit; do not reject the gift of the card in this realm for it speaks to you of immortality and the verdancy of spring in your soul.

6. Realm of Terrors: challenges to overcome. What is the source of strength in your life?

The Realm of Terrors holds few terrors for you. Your doubts and uncertainties were the only monsters here. You have measured yourself against them and found them wanting. Look again at the card that lies here; does it speak to you of a challenge you have not yet met, of a lurking fear that may possibly become a strength? Befriend it and let it teach you your full potential.

7. The Realm of Heart's Desire: beauty and harmony. What is the source of inspiration in your life?

The Realm of Heart's Desire, as you have discovered, is a place of painful pleasure. What you sought as an ideal solution, as a longed-for dream, sometimes looks wrong close-up, not what you wanted at all. If the *immram* has taught you any-

thing, it has helped you sift the insubstantial desires from the true ones. Do not be dazzled by unworthy desires, but reach down deep and find your heart's treasure. Take the gift of this realm with you into your own world and let its beauty shine in dark places.

8. Realm of Many Colours: change and possibility. What is the source of versatility or adaptability in your life?

The Realm of Many Colours shows you your original difficulty or problem. What power did it have to make you begin this voyage? Does it still exercise power over you, or has the balance shifted? The Realm of Many Colours is one of great possibility, yet many neglect its gifts by remaining narrowly blinkered on their own concerns. The *immram* you have taken may have helped you shift your perceptions from yourself and given you a fresh perspective.

9. Harbour: foundation and establishment. What gift or opportunity does your present position give to you?

The Harbour is the place of your home, where you will be established. At the end of every voyage, it is necessary to take stock and determine the future use of your freight. This card position urges you to re-evaluate your resources and the lessons you have learned on the *immram*.

ASPECTS OF READING THE CARDS

GETTING TO KNOW THE CARDS

It takes time and many readings to get to know the meanings of the cards. Use the book unashamedly to help until you get a feel of the cards. Meanwhile you will familiarize yourself with each card much more quickly if you play with the deck, without attempting to do a formal reading. Here are a few familiarization games to play.

1. Choose the card you like the most. Choose the card you like least. Choose one for which you feel

no particular liking or distaste. Set the three down and read the meanings. What does this tell you about yourself? Try this three-card spread with friends and family, for practice.

2. Take five cards from the pack, sight unseen, and lay them down in a line, in the order in which you draw them. Make up a story that connects all five. You do not have to use the meanings for this game, but just look at the images and let the story unfold.

3. Look through the pack and consciously choose cards that exemplify your current circumstances.

4. Plan an ideal *immram* for yourself, using the images, just as you would in a travel agency to plan a holiday. You can also choose cards that suggest solutions to current needs. When your itinerary is assembled, place the cards on the cloth and use creative day-dreams to enjoy your route.

5. In the evening, pick a card at random from the pack. Consulting the meaning, ask yourself in what ways has this card been an operative factor in your day today? In what ways has it been absent from your day?

HOW TO INTERPRET THE CARDS

In Chapter Three, you will find a full list of meanings. These may be read straightforwardly. But sometimes cards do not give their meanings very easily. For this reason, each meaning is followed by a challenge. The question underlying your *immram* should be read aloud and answered truthfully. The process of asking a question often unlocks a meaning hidden from the reader, and will sometimes deepen a reading that seems facile. In Chapter Five, there are some sample readings that you can study. Indecisive readings can be clarified by drawing a Gift Card.

When reading a single card you may be faced with a range of possible interpretations. Choose one that seems most apposite. Interpret each card separately according to its position, and be sensitive to the special meanings that may occur. Then assess the whole reading and see if there is any one feature that recurs. When reading for others or yourself, let the interpretation unfold like a story.

Certain *immram* cards are enhanced in meaning when they fall upon resonant realm positions. These are listed on the opposite page together with their very clear meanings. When these occur in either *Immram* One or Two, pay special attention to these positions. They represent an otherwordly message that should not be ignored.

You will probably initially use the cards for yourself, but you may be implored to give readings when others see them. By all means show them and pass them round in company, but it is usually better to do readings for another when you can be quiet together. Apart from anything else, the readings can often be very revealing and this might be embarrassing for your querent – the one asking the question of you, the reader. A private reading in quiet confidentiality is better by far.

Queries

What happens when cards appear in a reversed position?
The cards are designed to be read upright. If they are reversed, turn them upright.
What happens when a card of 'negative' import falls upon a 'positive' position?
The experiences represented within each card are neither negative nor positive, they just exist. Western society has fostered a very dualistic way of approaching everything, judging things to be 'good' or 'bad', frequently on a subjective basis. Rain may be perceived as 'bad' by tourists, for example, but 'good' by gardeners. Rain is neither good nor bad in itself.

We have only to look at the Island of Black and White, which directs us to look at reflection, to understand that such sudden reversals of perception happen frequently within the Otherworld and are nothing to worry about. When this happens you

THE MEANINGS OF CARDS IN SIGNIFICANT POSITIONS

REALM	CARD	CLEAR MESSAGE
Harbour	10. Island of the Cat 14. Island of Sorrow 30. Island of Joy	It is on these islands that the foster-brothers are lost. Abandon your *immram*. Read no further now but try later.
Realm of Many Colours	26. Island of the Shuttered Door	It is imperative that you now seize an opportunity.
Realm of Heart's Desire	31. Island of Circled Fire	Your dream can come true.
Realm of Terrors	1. Island of Giant Ants 22. Sea of Mist	There are challenges facing you that are greater than your present capabilities. Get help and advice before proceeding.
Realm of Youth	29. Island of the Eagle	Be prepared to transform your life. Great changes lie ahead.
Realm of Glass	21. Sea of Glass	Trust your intuitions now. You will rarely access these perceptions as clearly again.
Realm of Fair Women	27. Island of Women	You have discovered the perfect relationship/job/situation. Appreciate this respectfully.
Realm of Wonders	9. Island of Fiery Pigs 18. Island of the Ancestors 23. Island of Recognition	Access your deepest memories. Help lies buried within you.
Landfall	33. Island of the Falcon	You can reach journey's end with success.

should treat the card as a key to a door you have not yet approached. If, for example, you were to lay the Sea of Mist on the Realm of Heart's Desire, it might indicate that you need to lose your way and that a temporary disorientation or lack of focus might free you to win your heart's desire.

I am fearful of some of the cards and worry about their influence on my life

The cards have no special powers. None of them, even those with shocking images upon them, can harm or hurt you. Challenge should not be automatically understood as malignant. The *immram* cards are not predictive and do not influence your life-path, although they may indicate factors that are *already* operative within it.

Other methods of using the *immram* cards in greater depth are given in Chapter Six. Examples of readings are given in the next chapter.

CHAPTER FIVE

Charting the Voyage

May my form be exalted,
May my law be ennobled,
May my strength be increased,
May my tomb not be readied,
May I not die on my journey,
May my return be ensured to me.

Early Irish invocation for protection

This chapter gives a few sample readings, drawing on each of the reading methods outlined in Chapter Four. Personal details of the clients who consulted me have been altered, but their readings remain unchanged. There are many ways in which you can approach an *immram* reading. Be adaptable, taking into account the person for whom you are reading and the prevailing circumstances.

1. Richard

This reading is an example of *Immram* One: the Outward Passage.

Richard was a very thin and shy young man who had a history of failed relationships and short-lived jobs. I did not know him; he came to me through a mutual friend for a general reading. Richard drew the Ever-living Lady as his guide.

HARBOUR 10. **Island of the Cat**. Richard appeared to be in a difficult position where he was not free to act. Under his veneer of youthful reticence he seemed restless and unsettled.

REALM OF MANY COLOURS 21. **Sea of Glass**. The basis of Richard's *immram* was the need for clearer perception of his problem. The previous card, however, seemed to render him powerless to begin.

REALM OF HEART'S DESIRE 9. **Island of Fiery Pigs**. Richard desired above all to discover a proper balance in his life. On his own admission, he had passed up many opportunities that could give him a sense of purpose.

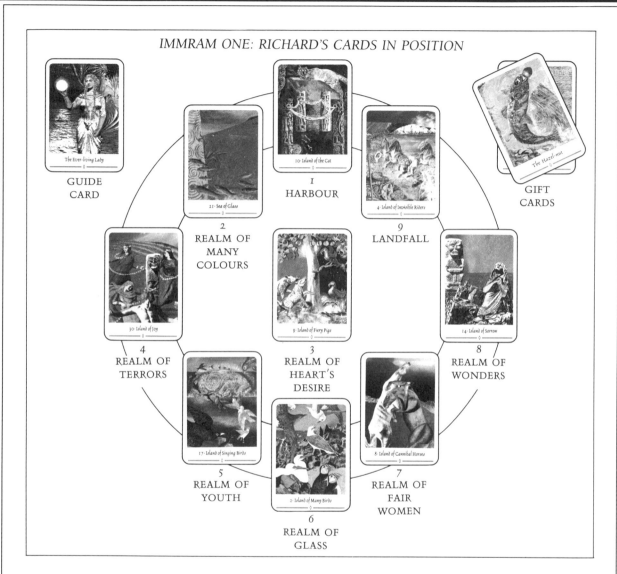

IMMRAM ONE: RICHARD'S CARDS IN POSITION

The Ever-living Lady

GUIDE
CARD

The Hazel-nut

GIFT
CARDS

10· Island of the Cat

1
HARBOUR

21· Sea of Glass

2
REALM OF
MANY
COLOURS

4· Island of Invisible Riders

9
LANDFALL

9· Island of Fiery Pigs

3
REALM OF
HEART'S
DESIRE

14· Island of Sorrow

8
REALM OF
WONDERS

30· Island of Joy

4
REALM OF
TERRORS

17· Island of Singing Birds

5
REALM OF
YOUTH

2· Island of Many Birds

6
REALM OF
GLASS

8· Island of Cannibal Horses

7
REALM OF
FAIR
WOMEN

REALM OF TERRORS 30. **Island of Joy**. This card represented not only a forbidden country to Richard but also one to which he was unable to travel due to some deep trauma. The juxtaposition of this card with the Realm of Terrors led me to question him more searchingly. I learned that he had been abused at an early age but had only admitted to this, prior to leaving college, to a friendly teacher. Although Richard had been in therapy, he had not stayed the course of treatment long enough to have brought about a transformational understanding of what had happened. He had been effectively cut off from his childhood innocence and joy by this experience.

REALM OF YOUTH   17. **Island of Singing Birds**. I felt that the talisman through this experience might well be music. Richard was a spare-time musician, playing for his own, rather than others' pleasure. For him, this was a source of inspiration that kept him going. Like Orpheus, Richard might yet find the strength to overcome the demons that lurked in his consciousness.

REALM OF GLASS   2. **Island of Many Birds**. Richard's progress had been hindered by a succession of people, both family and friends, proffering good advice as to how he should run his life. Although he had made friends since taking up his job, he had not kept a relationship for long.

REALM OF FAIR WOMEN   8. **Island of Cannibal Horses**. This card seemed to belie its position of 'help'. It appeared to me that Richard had been purposely sabotaging his chances, both in relationships and job prospects, and that the best help he could receive right now was to recognize this tendency. It was imperative that he faced up to the problems that dogged his steps.

REALM OF WONDERS   14. **Island of Sorrow**. The only vision that Richard could access at this time was the internal video of what had been done to him as a boy. It kept replaying itself in his consciousness so that he was as stuck upon the Island of Sorrow as Maelduin's foster-brother.

LANDFALL   4. **Island of Invisible Riders**. Richard needed to believe in himself in order to find his life's purpose, but that would be difficult to do without his lost childhood. I urged him to seek a resolution to his *immram* by facing the fact that he was a child-abuse *survivor*, and that he had to retrace his steps to make a conscious effort to comprehend, as a man, what had happened to him as a child.

SUMMARY   I felt helpless and humble in the presence of Richard who was just about able to get on with his life with so few resources to draw upon. When he went to draw a Gift Card, he pulled out two. He went to put one back, but something made me stop him. Perhaps he really did need two gifts, rather than one. The Apple promised him healing. The Hazel-nut offered him counsel and wisdom.

2. Diana

This reading is an other example of *Immram* One: the Outward Passage.

Diana was a young business woman who had recently been having a series of challenging confrontations. Although she was a person of resource and considerable verve, they were beginning to wear her down. She wanted to take an *immram* to find out just what was happening in her inner life to cause such provocation, and what might be done about it.

On my suggestion, she drew the Ever-living Lady, indicating that she was making a voyage from darkness into deeper illumination. When the spread had been laid out, this picture emerged.

HARBOUR   12. **Island of Giant Cattle**. Diana's present position was very much one of being overwhelmed. There was also a suggestion that she had provoked the various confrontations that had recently arisen, which she admitted might be true, since her approach was diametrically different from that of the other people involved. She seemed to have a very confrontational attitude to life in general.

REALM OF MANY COLOURS   2. **Island of Many Birds**.

There were altogether too many things happening at once. This was unsettling her to the extent that she had needed to seek advice. Her normally clear thoughts were like the cliff full of screaming birds, as depicted on this card.

REALM OF HEART'S DESIRE   10. Island of the Cat. Diana thought that her heart's desire was being able to keep many things in the air at once. There was a suggestion, however, that she might actually enjoy doing others out of their rightful reward, although she would not admit to this. I had suggested that she clarify this issue herself by looking deeply into her own motivations.

REALM OF TERRORS   21. Sea of Glass. Diana's impressive powers of perception had given her terrifying insights into the situation. She could see the factors that had gone into provoking the confrontations, and there was a sense of recoil at the mess things were in right now. This seemed linked with the preceding card and the fact that she was perhaps bringing trouble on herself by being overly critical of others.

REALM OF YOUTH   8. Island of Cannibal Horses. Diana's major strength lay in her powers of attack in a confrontational situation. I advised that she should not remain passive but draw upon these abilities in more skilful ways, resorting to arbitration rather than outright attack.

REALM OF GLASS   28. Island of Berries. The major irritant in Diana's current position was one particular man, her immediate superior in the company, whose expectations of her exceeded his knowledge of her past work-record. It was almost as though he had confused her with another person or was just plain forgetful of what the priorities really were. We suggested that she find ways of indicating to him the realistic background of the situation, possibly by enlisting the help of other colleagues.

REALM OF FAIR WOMEN   33. Island of the Falcon. Diana's chief consolation was the fact that the situation had an end in sight quite soon, since matters were coming to a head when something had to

break. I suggested that she begin to visualize the aftermath of this situation in a positive way that would help her acclimatize to the chances that might be on the horizon at work.

REALM OF WONDERS   19. Island of the Hermit. This card showed that Diana had sufficient resources to cope with the situation. It seemed likely that she would be offered another post, possibly from more than one company.

LANDFALL   18. Island of the Ancestors. By trusting to her own abilities and supportive frameworks, Diana would find her situation improving incrementally. This might mean a period of quiet establishment, but she said this would be welcome after the recent storms.

SUMMARY   This was quite a difficult reading due to the fact that more than one situation was operative in Diana's question. I tended to focus upon the confrontational nature of all these situations and allow the cards to determine the rest. Diana finally drew the Gift Card to receive the Silver Branch: this seemed to advise her to allow the heat to go out of the confrontational areas of her life and to draw upon the imaginative side of her life for healing and refreshment. The silver branch was traditionally shaken to bring silence or peace. Now, several months later, Diana seems to have reached a plateau in her working life. She has since had to cope with further confrontational encounters, but has drawn upon her Gift Card to help her find the way through. Her term of employment is at an end, due to the winding down of her company, and she is now actively searching for a mode of work where she will not be at the beck and call of employers. Her intentions are to find a home out of the city and to do private consultative work which will give her a quieter lifestyle.

3. Michael

This reading is an example of *Immram* Two: the Homeward Passage.

Michael was undergoing a lot of self-questioning. He had abandoned an artistic career in favour of a more lucrative job. His whole way of life seemed to be in the process of transformation and he wanted to clarify his direction.

He drew Barinthus, indicating that he was voyaging from the inmost self to a position of clarification and manifestation of his abilities.

LANDFALL   26. Island of the Shuttered Door. The homeward voyage for Michael was the use of his talents that he had been keeping to himself. He was modest about his accomplishments, often giving away work rather than accepting money for it. Practical application of his skills seemed paramount.

REALM OF WONDERS   25. Pillar of the Silver Net. This revealed that the root of Michael's transformation had been a profoundly spiritual, as well as vocational, call. He had discovered deeper access to his creative gifts. To some extent, he already had that valuable ability to trust the creative flow of his life.

REALM OF FAIR WOMEN   24. Island of the Rainbow Stream. This showed that Michael lived in true harmony with life, a reward in itself, providing a strong basis upon which he might build his new life-direction. It also became clear that the abandonment of his career had been due to the nature of the commissions he had received: he did not want to create what he considered unaesthetic art. Most commercial commissions had been of this nature.

REALM OF GLASS   23. Island of Recognition. Although Michael wanted to succeed creatively, he also had a misplaced modesty that caused him to shy away from the fact that his work might be acclaimed. I urged him to put these doubts aside and to concentrate upon the work that he wanted to do and was able to produce. This seemed to be at the root of the avoidance of his gifts.

REALM OF YOUTH   22. Sea of Mist. Michael's strength lay in working industriously while alone; indeed, he often seemed to produce work when in a state of confusion, and was able to clarify things in his mind this way. It struck me that he might have a talent for helping people by means of creative-arts therapy, and that he needed to work in a secure environment for his creative gifts to operate.

REALM OF TERRORS   28. Island of Berries. It was not surprising to find that Michael held himself back through his desire for obscurity and quietness, but he needed the reality of competition and acclaim. His greatest strength now lay in returning from his period of enforced rest and making a fresh start.

REALM OF HEART'S DESIRE   12. Island of Giant Cattle. Michael's heart's desire was to try a really large enterprise and succeed at it. It was obvious from speaking with him that the scope of his creative ability was ambitious. Perhaps this gave him a sense of 'showing off' and a subsequent sense of shame that made him discredit his work?

REALM OF MANY COLOURS   10. Island of the Cat. His immediate need was to get down and make a positive start. I suggested that he decide upon some goals, so that he started concentrating his energies purposefully. Caution, too, was necessary.

HARBOUR   9. Island of Fiery Pigs. Michael would come into harbour to the place and at the time most appropriate to him. He would certainly realize his goals and find his whole life renewed if he was able to find the necessary balance. The last two cards reinforced each other, suggesting that he should consider new art projects practically as a means of earning money, but not neglecting to address the deeper needs of his creativity.

SUMMARY   Michael drew the Dragon-stone Gift Card which gave him the strength to achieve his heart's desire. Michael has since moved and is sharing a flat

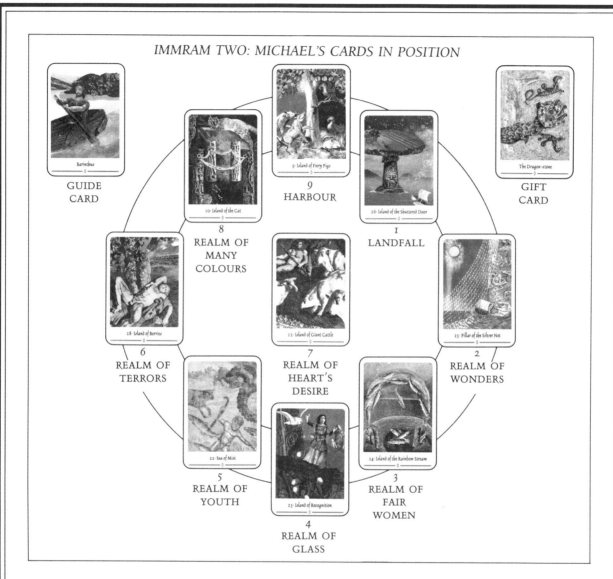

IMMRAM TWO: MICHAEL'S CARDS IN POSITION

GUIDE
CARD

Barinthus

GIFT
CARD

The Dragon-stone

9
HARBOUR

9 · Island of Fiery Pigs

I
LANDFALL

26 · Island of the Shuttered Door

8
REALM OF
MANY
COLOURS

10 · Island of the Cat

2
REALM OF
WONDERS

25 · Pillar of the Silver Net

7
REALM OF
HEART'S
DESIRE

12 · Island of Giant Cattle

6
REALM OF
TERRORS

28 · Island of Berries

5
REALM OF
YOUTH

22 · Sea of Mist

3
REALM OF
FAIR
WOMEN

24 · Island of the Rainbow Stream

4
REALM OF
GLASS

23 · Island of Recognition

with a friend. In other respects, his outer life seems unchanged but his spiritual commitment has led him to explore the inner worlds with deeper resolve. I feel that he has yet to find his niche in life.

the Furthest West

Come let us build the ship of the future
In an ancient pattern that journeys far.
Come let us set sail for the always islands,
Through seas of leaving to the Summer Stars.

'The Circle is Unbroken', song by Robin Williamson

The *immram* has many potential applications for practical use. This book has so far mainly explored the way of the inner quest for meaning, using the cards and the cloth as visual gateways. The *immram* can also be used in other ways, which will be the focus of this chapter. Shamanic journeying makes use of the *immram*, but takes the inner quest much deeper. Its possibilities are explored in detail in this chapter. I will also explain how *The Celtic Book of the Dead* can truly fulfil the purpose of its title by helping those facing death to make their preparation.

IMMRAM AS SHAMANIC JOURNEY

The *immram* cards can be used to help you explore the Otherworld, into which Maelduin sailed, in greater depth and first hand. The Shamanic journey is a method of inner journeying whereby the shaman travels in spirit to visit the Otherworld. The purpose is to find empowerment and assistance, to seek information and to help bring healing into the mundane realm. You may journey for any of these reasons, but primarily you may find it useful for restoring your purpose in life.

A shaman is a man or woman, usually of an indigenous spiritual tradition, who walks between the worlds as a healer, seeking to attune to the primordial resonances of the Otherworld and to retune those people and places that fall out of harmony. In most societies, the shaman was replaced by the priest. In the twentieth century, the priest began to be replaced by the analyst. Now the analyst, who works mainly in the psychological realms, and the priest, who works mainly in the spiritual realms, are being reminded by Native American, European, Asian and African shamans and healers that the body, psyche, mind and spirit must be encompassed within a single understanding.

The practical, psychic, mental and the mystical levels of each human being need to be fully operative once again, just as they were among the Celts. Their shamans were the poets, story-tellers and druids – wise men and women who understood the unity of the self within the framework of life. They blessed the day's work at dawn with prayers, singing in harmony with the work at midday, and brought the work to its conclusion at sunset with a chant of joy. In the stillness and darkness of the night, they were remade.

Darkness is not evil: it is the dimension into which we pass to rest and be restored. Death is the night of life, wherein life may be transformed. Similarly, the darkness of doubt, uncertainty or unknowing are states wherein we strive to recover the light of direction, certainty and knowledge. It is into this unknown realm of darkness that the ship of the *immram* sails to guide the soul. This makes the *immram* a wonderful way in which to enter states of uncertainty, whether they be about the problems of life or to prepare the way for death, for it gives us a map by which to steer. The *Voyage of Maelduin* thus constitutes a non-religious yet traditional framework of spiritual exploration and inner voyaging. Different stories convey different forms of wisdom and teaching, as we saw in Chapter One. The *immrama* give knowledge of the unknown and share the wisdom of transition and transformation. These can be used by anyone in a shamanic way, for shamanism in the twenty-first century will span the spiritual divides that beleaguered our immediate ancestors and bring us into a more wholistic universal relationship.

Why make a shamanic journey? Shamanic traditions from all over the world show that, at certain critical points in their lives, many people need to clarify their own condition. They may need physical or psychological healing, they may have lost their purpose, their delight in living, or they may need a new sense of direction before their lives are harmonious once more. To effect these realizations, shamans of all traditions conduct their client on an otherworldly journey to visit empowering beings, totems of many species, the ancestors or the gods. In shamanic traditions of both North and South America, as well as within Celtic tradition, the journey often takes the form of a voyage.

The shaman drums, rattles or chants the client into the Otherworld and guides him/her to the place in alternative reality where the empowering beings are encountered. The client is then conducted safely back, once more connected with what makes his/her life purposeful. Often the shaman will journey alone, on behalf of a client. Few modern people have the opportunity to partake of such journeys, despite the growing numbers of white Westerners who are becoming professional shamans. There follows a simple method of experiencing the otherworldly realities that the individual reader can perform alone.

EMBARKING UPON YOUR JOURNEY

Taking a shamanic journey involves meditative visualization. You do not travel with your body but with your spirit, visualizing and following the successive images that arise. This is not self-projected, as in day-dreaming; neither is it exactly like dreaming, nor a guided-imagery meditation. You may be familiar with the last method, which involves listening to someone reading the text of a scenario and allowing the images to rise. Shamanic journeying is much more open-ended than this, for there is no script to which you respond. You travel with intention, having decided beforehand to where you wish to journey and for what reason. Your journey will therefore be deeply personal. When using this book, however, you will have a good idea of where you are bound because the *Voyage of Maelduin* has already mapped out the sequence of the otherworldly journey.

Shamanic journeying is facilitated by the practitioner listening to the steady, rhythmic beat of a drum or rattle. Such repetitive sound enables you to concentrate with your consciousness, which is not the same as concentrating with your mind. Your mind does not direct this journey although it may observe and interpret the images that occur. During a journey you are tuning your whole being to the otherworldly mode. To this end, the drumming helps steady your heartbeat, allowing the body to relax, the busy mind to be stilled and the spirit to become alert. Please note that shamanic journeying is not accomplished with the help of popular music, however rhythmic the beat! Specific rhythms are needed to sustain the journey, and a definite 'call-back' signal is required so that you are restored to normal, everyday consciousness once again. To obtain a shamanic tape of drumming *see* Resources on page 136.

Decide where you are going to journey by taking the appropriate card/s. Find out which islands relate to your issue by working with the meanings given in Chapter Three, or the further correlations to the islands found later in this chapter. Give yourself time and space to be undisturbed. Allow the drumming to help you begin a voyage. Close your eyes and visualize the journey. At first, you may have difficulty visualizing, but your ability will improve with practice. Beginners will also find that it is better to journey to only one island at a time. It helps if you visualize the scenes as though you were enacting them, rather than visualizing yourself doing them as on a television screen. Your aim is to have immediate and personal experience. Approach your island and step ashore. Imaginatively explore the island, using the printed image only as a gateway or door through which you step. Meet and greet any beings upon the island. Question them and listen to their answers. The static, two-dimensional images on the cards will come to life, the

characters and beings of the Otherworld will speak to you. As well as the islands and beings depicted on the cards, you may discover others when you start to journey. If you approach an island that you regard as fearful or difficult, ask the beings or the land itself to show you their/its other side. The wrathful appearances of some beings are often to challenge the unwary; when they are approached respectfully, they will reveal other faces, answer questions and truly help you.

Some people are worried about what they see: is it real, are they imagining it, are they forcing the image to be there? The reality of the Otherworld, acknowledged by traditions the world over, may be difficult to accept when you have no personal knowledge of it. The first image you perceive will usually be the 'right' one for you; it is important to keep an open mind and prepare to be flexible. Every single person will have a different kind of experience when they journey, although certain basic experiences are consistent to all travellers. I suggest that, if you feel drawn to this work, you experiment with a good will and open heart. If it does not work for you, do not continue. It may be that in future times you will find the way in which you seek. There now follows, as an example of a shamanic journey, sample instructions for a journey to the Island of Giant Ants, and an interpretation.

Sample Journey Instructions

Be aware of the earth beneath you as you prepare to travel. Listening to the drum-beat, begin to visualize the sea and your ship. Sail from the shore towards the Island of Giant Ants. You have come to learn from these insect totems: you may ask questions about fears that you have and about tasks you are planning or working on right now. If the ants frighten you, ask them to reduce in size and ferocity. Listen to their wisdom, exploring this island further if it seems appropriate. Return to your own time and place by visualizing a return voyage. Feel the ground beneath you and slowly open your eyes.

Record your findings and experiences. If you feel disorientated, earth yourself by drinking and eating, and affirm your return to your own world.

Sample Report on this Journey

'I had no difficulty visualizing the boat that was pulled up on the shore. I stepped in and the boat took me off towards the horizon. It was rather frightening being alone at sea, as I am not a good swimmer. The Island of Giant Ants appeared before me and I stepped ashore onto the sand. The beach was surrounded by scrubby bushes. The ants were doing a kind of dance when I first saw them. Then they saw me and froze into watchfulness. I greeted them, rather cautiously, and asked them to help me. They came and "smelled" me with their antennae. Although I am not worried by insects, these were very large indeed, the size of Shetland ponies. I took several deep breaths and told them that I needed their help to organize my work in a better way. They listened carefully, then got very excited and bore me off over the ridge. Here there were flat, round pebbles all piled up. They put their heads together and began to rearrange the stones. When they finished, I saw that each stone had one work component marked on it and that the pebbles were organized in a sevenfold pattern. At first I did not understand, then I saw that it was arranged as a week of seven days. I also noticed a pile of unused stones and turned these over to see what was written on them. They seemed to be projects I had been struggling to schedule into my work-load. There were also several other components of my life that I now realize are probably inessential. I asked about these and they said that, if humans were like ants, I would have had lots of help to integrate these tasks but that I could not do so much on my own. I thanked them and set off back home.'

THE FOUR WORLDS

In the diagram on page 119 we see the *Voyage of Maelduin* arranged as a spiral journey. It was only in the closing stages of researching this book that this pattern became clear to me, for though I realized that the route Maelduin takes draws him deeper and deeper into the Otherworld, its overall shape and meaning remained obscure to me. As soon as I placed each of the islands on the fourfold spiral circuit of the eight-spoked wheel, the pattern and significance became obvious.

The symbol of the spiral is found throughout the Celtic World, both in art as well as in spiritual practice. Irish pilgrims still make a *deosil* or sunwise circuit of sacred places today, while saying special prayers. At each 'station' or resting place, they recite prayers and make visualizations. Although the ancient prayer-forms have mostly now been forgotten and replaced with the recitation of the rosary, the continuation of this practice testifies to its importance within the spiritual journey of the pilgrim who spirals within to discover deeper levels of reality.

By using the methods of shamanic journeying given at the beginning of this chapter, as well as in other ways described below, you can explore this spiral progression. The purpose of journeying in this way is to explore the potentialities of the Celtic Otherworld in an active and intentional way by experiencing the islands at first hand.

A full shamanic exploration of each island will take a long time and might not be appropriate for everyone. Those new to shamanic work might wish to read the explanations below in full before attempting any journey, then to choose consciously an itinerary for themselves in the following way.

Select four islands, one from each of the Four Worlds, that concern issues you would like to address personally. Visualize your voyage. Journey in sequence, starting within the Totemic World and voyaging to the Deep World. Visit each of your chosen islands; encounter its inhabitants, then return to your boat. Continue until you reach the last island of your choice. Visualize your return voyage home by the shortest passage. Write down your findings and realizations.

Those who would like to explore the entire spiral should journey in sequence, but return after visiting no more than six to eight islands. After several sessions you will have travelled through the whole spiral. A more advanced form of journeying can be performed when you are totally familiar with the full sequence of islands and the kinds of experience encountered on each one. You might, for example, wish to journey for the purpose of discovering the best use of your skills and talents; this might involve journeying to some of the islands that concern potential and vocation, such as the Islands of Trees, Giant Cattle, Four Fences, Singing Birds, Forge and the Shuttered Door, to see what insights await you there. But before we begin any travelling, let us examine this map of the Otherworld in detail.

THE IMMRAM AS A MAP OF THE OTHERWORLD

Each cycle of the spiral gives a different experience, and corresponds to one of the cosmological realms:
Cycle A, the Totemic World, represents the realm of earth and relates to the body.
Cycle B, the Vision World, represents the realm of the moon and relates to the psyche.
Cycle C, the Elemental World, represents the realm of the sun and relates to the soul.
Cycle D, the Deep World, represents the realm of the stars and relates to the spirit.

CYCLE A: The Totemic World

This cycle gives experience of the totems and dif-ferent species that comprise the Otherworld. Totems are emblematic life forms that archetypally represent the powers of their species within the Otherworld. Tribal and native peoples in Australia, New Guinea, northern Europe and the Americas, who live in close proximity to the Otherworld, often have personal animal or plant totems whose nature and qualities they mystically share. The totems are also said to teach us about the Otherworld and act as companions and helpers. In the *immram* they act as challengers and guardians of the otherworldly thresholds. They are not the same as the animals that inhabit our world. The Totemic World is ruled by the planet Earth; it teaches us about mundane life on a level we can comprehend: through our body. The eight different species in this cycle each gives experience of the Totemic World. Each species has its own myriad of gifts and qualities. Here, only the generalized gifts of each species are noted.

1. Island of Giant Ants: lore of insects

While the well-ordered, hierarchical structure of the beehive is generally admired by humans because of its by-product honey, the similarly well-organized society of the ants is less appreciated. Perhaps this is because the ants' nest is often seen as a microcosm of industrial and urban life. The insect totems have much to teach us about the patterns of life, attention to detail and faithfulness and commitment to our tasks.

2. Island of Many Birds: lore of birds

The miracle of birds and their adaptability to our world is extraordinary. Their ability to fly gives them perspectives that we can never have. The bird totems teach us to break down barriers, alerting us to the presence of danger and encouraging us to seek the deep messages of the Otherworld. They give us the gift of psychic communication and open to us the gifts of the airways.

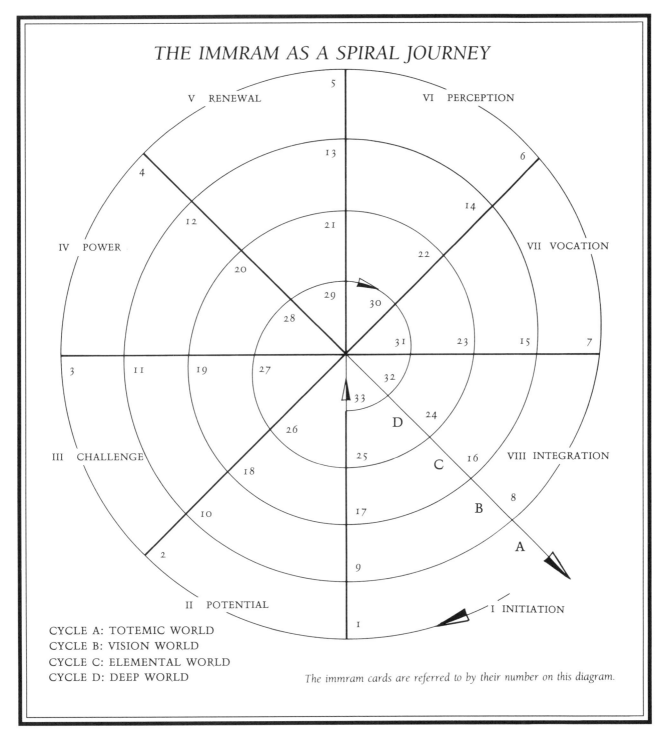

THE IMMRAM AS A SPIRAL JOURNEY

V RENEWAL

VI PERCEPTION

IV POWER

VII VOCATION

III CHALLENGE

VIII INTEGRATION

II POTENTIAL

I INITIATION

CYCLE A: TOTEMIC WORLD
CYCLE B: VISION WORLD
CYCLE C: ELEMENTAL WORLD
CYCLE D: DEEP WORLD

The immram cards are referred to by their number on this diagram.

3. Island of the Hound-footed Horse: lore of mammals

Our world's variety of mammals is decreasing rapidly as their habitats are colonized for human use. Nearest to human beings in nature, they are our most immediate teachers. The mammalian totems teach us a variety of skills including swift instinct, strengths of many kinds and communion with the earth.

4. Island of Invisible Riders: lore of otherworldly beasts

Otherworldly totems are included here because they have played an important part in our cultural development and mythic imagination. Dragons, unicorns, kelpies and salamanders are but a handful of the variety of mythic beasts that inform us of the Otherworld. Their beauty and strangeness teach us to value the high virtues of beauty, honour, compassion, harmony and power.

5. Island of Plenteous Salmon: lore of fish

The pollution of our waters endangers many aquatic creatures. The fish totems nevertheless teach us speed and serendipidy, strengthening our intuitive senses. They also give us the ability to utilize the gifts of water.

6. Island of Trees: lore of trees

The vegetable kingdom is represented here by the apple tree. Trees are the royalty of the plant world. Of their many gifts, they show us stability, fruitfulness and connection with the many inner worlds. The tree connects the Underworld, our own world and the Upperworld or Otherworld.

7. Island of the Revolving Beast: lore of reptiles

Although the card depicts a mammalian animal, the revolving beast represents the transformative richness of reptilian life. The reptiles teach us stealth, patience and the ability to transform ourselves.

8. Island of Cannibal Horses: lore of humans

Human beings are not normally considered to be totems, yet they appear, by extension, in the image of the cannibal horses. Real horses do not act this way; such predatory behaviour is that of humankind. Human beings consider themselves the supreme life form, but the salutary thought remains that life may not stop its evolutionary spiral. Perhaps to life forms yet to come, the human will appear in totemic guise. What totemic gifts would humankind offer these beings? The ability to adapt, create and imagine might serve as the beneficial gifts of humankind.

CYCLE B: The Vision World

This cycle gives experience of deep dreams and visions that mirror our own mundane world. Dreams and visions often reveal to us things we would rather not know about or have been avoiding. This world is under the rulership of the moon, which acts as Earth's companion. Its patterns and cycles, although they appear to be mutable, follow a prescribed shape. When we come to terms with the cycles of our own life, we have a better grasp of both inner and outer travelling. The Vision World teaches us through our psyche, the impressionable reflector of the transient light of the moon.

9. Island of Fiery Pigs: vision of balance

The beauty of this image with its interrelated species co-existing harmoniously and drawing their nourishment from the same tree, is a valuable lesson in balance. Balance is often based on reciprocation, generosity and tolerance, qualities that typify this Vision World.

10. Island of the Cat: vision of respect

Much of our world is without respect for other living beings. Every sentient being is possessed of the spark of life and of an eternal soul. To obscure the soul of another is to steal its light. Respect is the opposite of theft: it recognizes and enhances the light in another.

11. Island of Black and White: vision of opposites

The lesson of this island is startling for it reverses our inherent views on things. So shocking is this experience that it has the effect of helping us to see with the eyes of others. The ultimate result is loss of selfishness, which keeps us bound and limited within our own frame of reference.

12. Island of Giant Cattle: vision of boundaries

Like the preceding island, this one also gives us insight into our own frameworks. It is helpful to know that we can go beyond our set limits and achieve great things; it is also important to know where our limits are. The lesson here is about pride and over-confidence. There are natural limits beyond which it is not wise to venture.

13. Island of the Mill: vision of generosity

The mill teaches us about openness of heart. We seek to possess, wanting everything to belong to us alone; but we cannot store goods, thoughts or feelings without imbalance. These things become our prison cell in which we are condemned to circulate. We need to find ways to relinquish our possessive nature and give generously of our time and resources without reserve.

14. Island of Sorrow: vision of loss

This vision of loss is one of the features of mortality that enables us to learn through sorrow and afflic-tion. It therefore seems strange to encounter the sharpest scourge of mortality in these immortal realms, yet life is reflected in all its appearances here. The wounds dealt by loss are difficult to com-prehend or accept, and yet we must each work towards a balanced acceptance that does not fall into hopeless resignation. The virtues that may accrue from suffering have been much vaunted and

are difficult to discern when we are sorrowful; yet this island may teach us their worth. These virtues are enduring strength, a peaceful heart and a com-passionate spirit.

15. Island of the Four Fences: vision of vocation

The ability to know our life's purpose is critical to our development as human beings. Vocation is not just about our daily employment, it is also about our spiritual direction. Each day, we must assess whether we are fulfilling our life's purpose. To find what it should be, we may inquire here.

16. Island of the Crystal Keep: vision of dreams

The vision of our dreams informs us of the deep messages of the Otherworld. Not all dreams tell us messages. The muddled recapitulations of a busy day may only tell us to leave some space for organic reflection in our lives. The deep, urgent dreams that come to us are teachers of importance.

CYCLE C: The Elemental World

This cycle reveals the lore of the elements and gives fundamental teachings about the Otherworld. The Elemental World is ruled by the sun, the star of our galaxy from which we derive light, heat and life. The elements referred to here are not the gross elements of air, fire, water and earth, but their subtle counterparts. This is the realm of archetypes where knowledge is the shaper. The teachings of this cycle take us yet deeper into the realm of the soul, the vessel of our essential self. The islands of this cycle represent the archetypal components of this essential self: when we have truly attuned our-selves to their modes, we will become mediators of the elements in mundane reality.

17. Island of Singing Birds: knowledge of the soul

Within each of us is an inner voice: it is called the conscience, the soul, the inner guide and many other names. Whatever we call it, that inner voice prompts us and shows us the way. When we make mistakes, it is often because we have ignored the inner voice. We need the stillness of silence in order to hear what the soul says. Attunement spaces should be made each day, so that we gain knowledge of the soul.

18. Island of the Ancestors: knowledge of the earth

The qualities of the earth are endurance, stability and abundance. All life is composed of ensouled matter. When the soul flees, the matter is returned to earth, to mingle with it. The Celts believed that the ancestral realms were beneath the earth and that the accumulated knowledge of the earth was accessible in the Underworld. If it is uncontrolled within us, the gifts of earth can manifest as stubbornness, fixity and miserliness. The earth teaches us patience and nourishes us.

19. Island of the Hermit: knowledge of the spirit

When the soul is properly attuned, which rarely happens in everyday life, we are sometimes given knowledge of the spirit. This happens usually in brief flashes of enlightenment, for while the soul is growing in strength it cannot bear too much exposure to the piercing light of the divine. The spirit usually comes to us in the shape of a known image or being who offers us the teachings of spiritual empowerment, but it may also come in other, unseen ways.

20. Island of the Forge: knowledge of fire

The qualities of fire are light, ardour and warmth. The fires of life run within our veins and give us our creativity. Uncontrolled fire can manifest as oppression of others, anger and destructive criticism. Fire teaches us control and kindles our enthusiasm.

21. Sea of Glass: knowledge of water

The qualities of water are love, purity and fertility.

Our body is predominantly composed of water. Uncontrolled water manifests as destructive emotion, polluted channels of communication and dryness of heart or spirit. Water teaches us trust and quenches our spiritual thirst.

22. Sea of Mist: knowledge of air

The qualities of air are life, liberty and inspiration. Breath inspirits our body giving it the gift of life. It is a gift we cannot refuse, since the only alternative is a suicidal act of suffocation. Uncontrolled air manifests as a narrow outlook on life, as limitation and a dispirited attitude. Air teaches us attention and blows away stale and outworn states.

23. Island of Recognition: knowledge of the mind

The mind is a fertile storehouse of interesting and irrelevant thought. Our society places great emphasis on mentation and reason, but it is a deeper quality of mind that we seek here. This island teaches and stimulates memory. As we catch the hazel-nut that is thrown in our direction, we may recall many memories that have been lost to us and our generation.

24. Island of the Rainbow Stream: knowledge of the heart

Knowledge of the heart is not related to the physical organ in our chests, but rather about innate understanding that cannot be learned through the senses or through the mind. This island teaches us the harmony and beauty of non-duality, where nothing is separate from any other being or thing. As in the Island of the Hermit, understanding may come to us only in brief flashes of comprehension, but we are bidden to recall the full gamut of teachings of the Elemental World in order to pass from this cycle into the next

CYCLE D: The Deep World

This cycle reveals the essential nature of the

Otherworld and provides opportunities for deep communion with it. The Deep World is ruled by the stellar realm. We note that, the further into the Otherworld we travel, the deeper we voyage into the stellar realms. Here the wisdom of the Otherworld is stored and freely available; those who journey this far are enabled to find their heart's desire and may, literally, 'wish upon a star'. The Deep World teaches us through the spirit, the state of total non-duality, of union with the divine.

25. Pillar of the Silver Net: wisdom of trust

This Pillar is a landmark upon the shamanic journey, bidding us to remember that, beyond it, we must live according to the rules of the Otherworld. This means learning to trust with strong faith. Trust and confidence are often shattered in the mundane world and are hard to rebuild. The Otherworld does not lie or deceive. At this deep level, we sail confidently, guided by the light of the stars.

26. Island of the Shuttered Door: wisdom of power

We are called upon to become empowered by exploring this island. Entering into our power with authority requires the trust we gained at the last staging post. Any doubt will cause the shuttered door to be closed in our face. This island is immensely important to people now alive: many are possessed of great resources that they could give to the world, but are uncertain. The power to explore this island is first learned on the Island of the Four Fences in the Vision World.

27. Island of Women: wisdom of love

Power without love is worthless. This island teaches the wisdom of reciprocal love. Love's exchange happens on many levels, not just in sexual union, although this serves to teach human beings the nonduality of spiritual awareness. Love is unbounded by time, space or dimension and so is one of the most powerful wisdoms this journey has to teach. Love spills over into all the worlds and heals the wounds of each.

28. Island of Berries: wisdom of dreams

The message of dreams was first attended to in the Vision World on the Island of the Crystal Keep; now it attains its full potential. The wisdom of dreams is fulfilled by prophecy and seership, the true gifts of the stars that govern this Deep World. To voyage by dreams alone requires the trust, power and love of the preceding islands. These may be not only the dreams of our sleeping life but also those of our waking life. The Island of Black and White may be called upon to help us access the opposite halves of our inner and outer existences.

29. Island of the Eagle: wisdom of re-creation

The power to remake and reshape ourselves is the lesson of this island. When we have achieved this transformation, we discover that this is but the microcosmic promise of greater transformation. We learn that we can be co-creators and shapers with the divine, that we each have power to re-create our own world.

30. Island of Joy: wisdom of joy

The riches of our human life come in many different kinds of experiential coinage. Joy, the most valuable coin in our pockets, cannot be hoarded for it turns to dust if it is not immediately shared. The wisdom of joy is not about unintentional hilarity or the telling of jokes; rather it is an abiding aspect of the spiritual realms that, like love, spills over into every world.

31. Island of Circled Fire: wisdom of peace

The gifts of this cycle combine to produce the innocent child of peace. Peace is the most longed-for of wisdoms and the most difficult to obtain, for it cannot manifest unless there is true will. To enter the realm of peace and bring its gifts back to our own world requires perfect trust, power devoid of self-interest, a heart full of compassionate love and dreams of re-creation and joy.

32. Island of Otters: wisdom of freedom

With the wisdom of peace resting gently upon us, we are able to attain freedom from the wheeling spirals of our voyaging. Freedom of spirit is attained when there is no desire to attach ourselves to our goal. It enables us to return to our own time and place where the many gifts and teachings we have obtained in the Otherworld can be applied to everyday reality.

THE LAST ISLAND: a recapitulation of the *immram*

33. Island of the Falcon: quest for the self

The quest for the self is both the goal of the journey and the journey itself. Monitoring our progress gives us opportunities to assimilate what we have learned on the voyage. It is all very well to receive the empowerments of lore, vision, knowledge and wisdom, but it is difficult to keep these ever before us. We therefore need to 'forget' them, as a gardener 'forgets' during the winter the seeds planted in the earth. The work of the seasons, like the exigencies of life, will bring these empowerments to natural germination when the time is ripe. All we have to do is remain attuned to our ideals, and watch for those first signs of germination. This way the lore, vision, knowledge and wisdom grow in our own native earth, rather than in foreign, otherworldly fields.

THE EIGHT PATHWAYS

The Spiral Journey diagram is divided into eight segments. Each segment, indicated by a Roman numeral, has a special significance. The islands that occur within each segment are interrelated in nature, yet each has a different intensity depending on within which of the Four Worlds it falls. These eight segments are like pathways of light that shine across our spiral journey to the depths of understanding. If we take as an example segment VI, the Pathway of Perception, we see that the islands occurring there relate to the way we view experience. In the Vision World, our perception is symbolized by the Island of Sorrow; by the time we have reached the Deep World, that perception has shifted entirely, being symbolized by the Island of Joy. Likewise, the Pathway of Challenge (segment III) presents us with the fearful test of the Hound-footed Horse in the Totemic World, while by the time we reach the Deep World, the testing is of a more subtle kind on the Island of Women. Each of the Eight Pathways is briefly explained here with reference to the islands that fall within its illuminating brilliance; you might find it useful to look at the cards as you read these definitions.

I INITIATION

Each of these islands is an initiation into a new cycle of experience. The ways in which we initiate that exploration are very important. Island 1 is a terrifying initiation to the journey, while Islands 9, 17 and 25 give us a fresh confidence. There can be no easy way of beginning the inner journey; it immediately confronts us with ourselves.

1. **Island of Giant Ants**: initiates by shock tactics; we are confronted by our fears and unwilling to continue.

9. **Island of Fiery Pigs**: initiates us into the ways of balanced living.

17. **Island of Singing Birds**: initiates us into recognizing the connections in our lives.

25. Pillar of the Silver Net: initiates us into the inner worlds with confidence.

II POTENTIAL

Each of these islands explores the nature of potential and the kinds of resources we each have. Island 2 gives us sustenance to encourage our further seeking; in exchange, we must access our own potential and not try to steal what we have not yet accessed for ourselves – the lesson of Island 10. Each person is genetically programmed with data and memories that have to be discovered and developed.

2. Island of Many Birds: reveals the potential of the Otherworld.

10. Island of the Cat: reveals the potential treasury of relationship that opens when we practise respect.

18. Island of the Ancestors: reveals the potential to be gained from ancestors, native traditions and wisdom of the earth.

26. Island of the Shuttered Door: reveals hidden potential awaiting discovery in the Deep World.

III CHALLENGE

The challenges we meet on the *immram* upset our preconceived notions of how things should be. They also send us back to the roots of our being to discover the truth. These challenges make us uncomfortable and none of these islands proves a place where travellers can stay for long: they usually flee or are asked to leave. Challenges are teachers. If we pass up challenges, they will keep recurring in our lives until we finally face them.

3. Island of Hound-footed Horse: challenges our perceptions.

11. Island of Black and White: challenges our prejudices and shows us the other side of the divide.

19. Island of the Hermit: challenges our inner resources and shows us other forms of spiritual nourishment.

27. Island of Women: challenges us to test our desires and to discover the wisdom of love.

IV POWER

Each of these islands is about issues of power, how we use it and respond to it. All these islands prove too strong for mortal travellers, who must find their own ways to cope with the power found there. It is not until Island 28 that Maelduin learns to dilute the power appropriately.

4. Island of Invisible Riders: shows us the power of the Otherworld.

12. Island of Giant Cattle: shows us the power of appropriate actions and how inappropriate behaviour creates division.

20. Island of the Forge: shows us the power of our skills and the fire of creativity.

28. Island of Berries: helps us to find our true power by dint of dreams, and insights that come when we are unaware.

V RENEWAL

Each of these islands explores renewal and clarification. Unless we are continually reborn or transformed upon the spiritual journey, we cease to move; we enter a stasis where nothing ever happens to us. These islands are in the opposite segment to those of Initiation and, like them, represent significant staging posts where restoration occurs.

5. Island of Plenteous Salmon: renews us by physical nourishment.

13. Island of the Mill: transforms our grudging into generous giving.

21. Sea of Glass: clarifies our perceptions through the renewing qualities of water.

29. Island of the Eagle: alchemically renews us to become essentially perfect.

VI PERCEPTION

We perceive the teachings of our *immram* experiences through our physical senses, our thoughts and emotions and higher senses. The senses of taste, sight, hearing, smell and touch, as well as the functions of feeling and thinking, belong to the physical body and the everyday world. The higher senses of intuition and mystical perception belong to the psychic world or Otherworld.

6. **Island of Trees:** teaches us to perceive emotional maturity and gives us a taste of the Otherworld.

14. **Island of Sorrow:** teaches us to perceive our dependence by loss or removal of things or people we cherish.

22. **Sea of Mist:** teaches us to trust our instincts during times of uncertainty.

30. **Island of Joy:** teaches us to find the fount of spiritual joy within us.

VII VOCATION

These islands show us the motivating pathways that lead to all inner exploration. Finding our true vocation is a very important thing, not just our daily employment, but our sense of life's purpose. Taking an *immram* may also reveal the spiritual vocation. The inner traveller realizes that the two are really one vocation.

7. **Island of the Revolving Beast:** shows us our inability to settle to anything.

15. **Island of the Four Fences:** shows us the possible vocations awaiting us.

23. **Island of Recognition:** reveals to us our true vocation.

31. **Island of Circled Fire:** reveals how our vocation will affect and help others.

VIII INTEGRATION

These islands show the virtue of appropriate behaviour and way of life. The experiences of the *immram* are no use to the traveller who fails to integrate what he or she has learned. The long spiral journey is itself a period of assimilation; it gives us a clear insight into the way in which the soul's deepening experience leads to integration on all levels.

8. **Island of Cannibal Horses:** shows our inability

to integrate with others.

16. **Island of the Crystal Keep:** gives us dreams that help us integrate our motivations.

24. **Island of the Rainbow Stream:** gives us the integration of harmony and a true heart.

32. **Island of Otters:** gives us integration with all beings through simplicity and forgiveness.

Each of the Eight Pathways is balanced by one of the others:

INITIATION (I) leads us into the inner journey; the way out is found by INTEGRATION (VIII).

POTENTIAL (II) shows us the possibilities; we develop these and find our VOCATION (VII).

CHALLENGE (III) limits and educates us; we are stretched and find skilful adaptations by means of PERCEPTION (VI).

POWER (IV) fills us with dynamism; we are reborn and transformed by RENEWAL (V).

ADVANCED IMMRAM READINGS

The Four Worlds and Eight Pathways can be used in more advanced *immram* readings to help clarify readings and reveal their hidden depths. This method is as follows:

Step 1. Photocopy the diagram on page 119 so that you can plot the reading more easily.

Step 2. Choose your cards and place them on the cloth, using *Immram* One or Two. Interpret the reading as normal.

Step 3. Ring the relevant numbers of the islands visited in your reading on your photocopied sheet of the Spiral Journey.

Step 4. Note which of the Four Worlds and Eight Pathways these cards occupy, and interpret the cards according to the information given in this chapter.

Let us take the reading done for Richard on pages

108–110 as an example. The cards he drew were: 2. Island of Many Birds, 4. Island of Invisible Riders, 8. Island of Cannibal Horses, 9. Island of Fiery Pigs, 10. Island of the Cat, 14. Island of Sorrow, 17. Island of Singing Birds, 21. Sea of Glass, and 30. Island of Joy.

We see that three cards fell into the Totemic World, showing that Richard's foundation for maintaining the mundane business of living was based upon the insights of the lore of birds, otherworldly beings and humans. This revealed that he had the ability to relate to the insights of the Otherworld, but was prone to flee from committing himself deeply and to sabotage his chances. There was also the promise that he could rectify this by beginning to connect more strongly to the adaptability suggested by the Cannibal Horses card.

Three cards fell into the Vision World, showing that Richard was spending a lot of time struggling to understand the underlying meaning of his life by means of the visions of balance, respect and loss; these three issues alone were significant clues to his unspoken preoccupations. Richard had never been able to experience personally the balance promised in the Fiery Pigs card for his light had been diminished by his past experience of abuse; he was consequently still coping with the loss suggested by the Island of Sorrow.

Two cards fell in the Elemental World, showing that Richard was making an attempt to realize and express his soul. The Island of Singing Birds and the Sea of Glass revealed that he had rich sources of spiritual nourishment at hand, if only he could access them. His love of music, instanced by the Singing Birds card and his need to acknowledge spiritual thirst, were issues that he had yet to address fully.

Only one card fell in the Deep World – the Island of Joy – whose wisdom would remain latent in Richard until he dealt with the more mundane yet critical issues that kept his life in chains.

Turning to the distribution of cards upon the Eight Pathways, we see that two cards fell in the Pathway of Initiation, offering Richard the possibillty of a more balanced and connected life-style. Two cards also fell in the Pathway of Potential, showing that he needed to release his innate gifts of otherworldly insight and reciprocal trust.

There was one card each in the Pathways of Power and Renewal, showing that Richard needed to acknowledge his ability to attune to the Otherworld as a real manifestation of his power; the Sea of Glass card suggested renewal, by means of mental clarity and purification.

Two cards fell in the Pathway of Perception: significantly the Islands of Sorrow and Joy. These showed that Richard's current dependency upon his perception of past sorrows could be transformed into joy if he was able to change his viewpoint. The one card falling in the Pathway of Integration revealed Richard's inability to integrate with the human race at large.

Significantly, Richard had no cards in the Pathways of either Challenge or Vocation, indicating that he was not confronting the serious issues underlying his problem; this in turn was keeping him from applying himself to his life's purpose.

A run of cards is often highly significant. Richard had Islands 8, 9 and 10, showing that his current focus was concerned with dealing with the abuse he had suffered in the past, with gaining a new balance and a true restoration of his childhood innocence.

This method of deeper interpretation and clarification can be applied to both reading methods given in Chapter Four. Instead of or as well as using the method above, you might wish to take a personal shamanic visualization. Start your journey at the lowest-numbered card you have drawn and journey to each island in the numerical sequence of the Spiral Journey, meeting and learning from the inhabitants of these islands. This is a good way to learn about the shape of your *immram* at first hand.

IMMRAM AS SOUL-LEADING

The *immram* has a very important application that is urgently needed at this time. In its scramble to acquire the art of living better, Western society has lost the art of dying. Very few of us have seen a dead person, fewer have seen anyone die and most of us make no preparation for death. The hospice movement, spearheaded by Elisabeth Kübler-Ross, has shown how the dying may do so with greater dignity and meaning.

The original Books of the Dead tried to prepare people for the inevitability of death so that fear of the unknown would be lessened. It is not surprising to learn that Celtic tradition has its own spiritual practices relating to the art of dying. These may be combined with practical use of the *immram* to enable the process of death to take place in a skilful and compassionate way.

In Scots Gaelic tradition, the body is understood to be the 'soul-shrine'. Before sleep, the angels are implored to keep the soul-shrine safely, as in this soul-shrine prayer that addresses the guardian angel:

> Be Thyself the guiding star above me,
> Illume Thou to me every reef and shoal,
> Pilot my barque on the crest of the wave,
> To the restful haven of the waveless sea.
> (Carmichael)

The bed itself therefore becomes like a boat, sailing through the land of dreaming or of death. This ancient understanding is borne out in the many burial customs of north-west Europe: votive ships have been found in graves and there is evidence of many boat burials, where the dead have been inhumed with their own boat, their spiritual vessel to the Otherworld.

This practice is related to the *Treoraich Anama* or soul-leading, whereby the dying person is conducted from this world to the other by a close friend:

> The soul peace is intoned, not necessarily by a cleric, over the dying, and the man or the woman who says it is called 'anam-chara' or soul-friend. He or she is held in special affection by the friends of the dying person ever after. The soul peace is sung slowly – all present earnestly joining the soul-friend in beseeching the Three Persons of the Godhead and all the saints of heaven to receive the departing soul of earth. During the prayer the soul-friend makes the sign of the cross with the right thumb over the lips of the dying. . . . When the person gives up the ghost the soul is seen ascending like a bright ball of light into the clouds.
> Then is said:
> 'The poor soul is now set free
> Outside the soul-shrine;
> O kindly Christ of the free blessings,
> Encompass thou my love in thine.'
> (ibid.)

The *immram* text may have originally been read aloud to the dying. This can be done today if the dying one has particular affinity with the Celtic world. It is not necessary to read through all parts of the text, but to select suitable islands. Those that may be particularly useful are those which sever the links between the dying one and conflicts he or she has suffered in this world: the Island of the Mill, for example, represents burdens and grudges that can be laid down. A modern method of soul-leading that can be used with suitable adaptations is suggested here. It is better if the person conducting this soul-leading is a family friend, minister or sympathetic acquaintance rather than a family member who may be too overwhelmed by grief, or a variety of emotions. The soul-friend becomes, in effect, a guide into the realms between and beyond.

There are many people who doubt the existence of any state beyond death. But anyone who has been at a deathbed will know that the dying one is often aware of another dimension beyond this earthly realm and that there *is* a wider frame of existence.

The following list of topics is equated with the Maelduin Voyage. It is intended for the use of those facing death or those acting as soul-friends for dying people. It is recommended that you re-read the full story and poem of the *Voyage of Maelduin* (*see* Chapter Two), and then read through the suggestions below, creating a suitable format for the needs of the dying person. Select appropriate islands and an itinerary; do not slavishly follow the order given here. The suggestions in brackets are instructions for guided-imagery journeys that the soul-friend will lead; adapt and explore these as possibilities.

1. Island of Giant Ants. Gently explore the nature of fear; the dying one's own fears may have changed or intensified with the approach of death.
2. Island of Many Birds. The daily round of life often assumes a new value as opportunities for living it grow fewer. Use this island to explore the old routines of getting and spending, of doing and preparing, and say farewell to them.
3. Island of the Hound-footed Horse. Old or untidy relationships may need resolution. Use this island to explore rejection, either offered or received by the dying one. It can also be a place to explore independence and co-dependence.
4. Island of Invisible Riders. The approach of death gives a new dimension to existence. Explore the different realms of being and of the unknown, using the dying one's own beliefs and concepts, if appropriate, or drawing upon existing afterlife scenarios that seem resonant.

5. Island of Plenteous Salmon. Self-nurture is a need that many people reject in the business of serving others. As death approaches, there may be many unfulfilled self-nurturing desires. Use this island to explore places, people, objects, actions etc. that the dying one wishes to visit, meet, see, do etc. (Go into the house and find something you need or desire at this time.)
6. Island of Trees. Taking nourishment may be restricted or difficult so it is important to nourish the dying one with everlasting food. Explore the kinds of cultural and spiritual fare of the dying one and make sure that opportunities for enjoying these are available daily.
7. Island of the Revolving Beast. The body's discomfort may be mirrored by the mind's torment or various anxieties. Use this island to check with the dying one where her or his essential self or soul is housed. You may find it valuable to draw upon Buddhist principles here. Meditation on this question may lead the dying one to discover that the body is not the only vehicle of existence. Use in conjunction with Island 4.
8. Island of Cannibal Horses. Self-torture or guilt is often deep-seated and hard to eradicate. Thoughts prey on the mind and go round and round in a wheel of pain. It is important to clear the way for death to occur. Explore the issues around guilt and encourage the dying one to relinquish it. Islands 13 and 32 can be used in conjunction with this one if a form of forgiveness or self-forgiveness is necessary.
9. Island of Fiery Pigs. This island provides an opportunity for the patterns and cycles of a lifetime to be considered dispassionately. Lead the dying one through the course of one day – dawn, noon, twilight, midnight – equating each to childhood, youth, adulthood and old age respectively, or to the length of life he or she has attained, and explore the

patterns within it. This will help give a sense of shape and life's purpose; the soul-friend may help by pointing to significant patterns if the dying one feels that life has been wasted.

10. **Island of the Cat.** At the approach of death, misappropriation of energies, things, time, emotions etc. often looms large. Lead the dying one into the house of treasures and visualize restoring to its proper place/owner the thing/energy that has been taken. Physical restoration of things or money may also be required and should be discreetly performed, if possible with the help of relatives. Restoration in kind, the giving of money to charity, for example, may help allay anxiety.

11. **Island of Black and White.** If the dying one has very fixed attitudes or prejudices that are obstacles to an easy death, lead him or her into the field of black and white to be helped over onto the opposite side of the fence, and experience how the other side/reversed position feels. Encourage a dialogue between the two entrenched positions, using objects or small figures to represent them, with the dying one vocalizing both sides of the dialogue.

12. **Island of Giant Cattle.** This island can be explored with relatives in mind. As death approaches, many loved ones are physically left behind. This is the place to explore ways of remaining in spiritual communion while being physically separated. (Visualize the fiery river as a fence and the meadow beyond as a place of peace and tranquillity. Both the living and dead may walk either side and speak to each other.) This visualization may be beneficial for relatives who have been unable to speak freely to the dying one and regret lost opportunity.

13. **Island of the Mill.** The dying have many burdens to lay down. Grudges, attachments and obligations may be worked out on this island. It is important to lay down our lifetime's luggage, for it will only hinder our swift passage. (Visualize entering the mill and seeing old grudges being ground down. Taking the grain, visualize going outside and

sowing it broadcast to the four winds as a free gift to all. As the winds take it, so do the burdens fall away.)

14. **Island of Sorrow.** Explore this island in conjunction with Island 30 and see them as opposite sides of the same coin. What is sorrowful for the bereaved is joyful for the dying one. These islands may be explored together by relatives and the dying one, so that each appreciates the needs of the other with greater understanding.

15. **Island of the Four Fences.** Untapped creative gifts and other unfulfilled areas of life are usually regretted by the dying one. Use this island to explore the many possibilities, roles and gifts that may be available in another incarnation (if the dying one accepts reincarnation as a possibility). Valuing the achievements of this life is also important, and should be noted by the soul-friend.

16. **Island of the Crystal Keep.** This is the island on which to explore the importance of dreams and inner promptings. (Encourage the dying one to relate a dream. Visualize the island, raise the slab and drink. Let her or him pass within the crystal keep with the woman and ask her about the dream's meaning. Help interpret the realizations.) This visualization can also be done for those who do not remember their dreams. Ask the dying one to visualize drinking from the deep well before sleeping and asking for remembrance of any dream that comes.

17. **Island of Singing Birds.** Music is profoundly helpful at the time of passing. Using the dying one's own preferences, explore this island with the help of music. (Visualize going to the island. Play the music, let the dying one listen and let the music lead him or her to an inner scenario. At the conclusion, let the dying one relate the journey; this may help subsequent *immrama* and be of benefit at the time of passing.)

18. **Island of the Ancestors.** Passing through death means saying goodbye and hello simultaneously. Use this island to meet with dead relatives, friends

or animals who have passed this way before. (Let the dying one ask those he or she meets if anyone is willing to act as a helper at the time of passing and then as a guide to the realm beyond death.)

19. Island of the Hermit. Here the soul-friend can explore the nature of dying, one's beliefs and spiritual inspirations. (Visualize an inspiring figure or spiritual being whom you respect, dispensing from the food well. Ask his or her help as a guide to lead you over. This need not be an acknowledged spiritual being, such as Christ or Moses; it might be the hero or heroine of a book, or anyone who inspires the dying one and gives him or her a sense of empowerment. The figure should be someone not now incarnate.)

20. Island of the Forge. Exploring the four elements is an ideal way of preparing for death. Each of the elements has been traditionally used to dispose of the dead body: inhumation in earth, cremation by fire, disposal in water and platform burial where the winds dry the body and predators dismember it. This island (or Islands 18, 21 or 22) may be explored with a burial service in mind. We can use these islands as places of changing. Fire is a great changer; use this island to help burn away what is no longer necessary. (Visualize the forge fire as a place of alchemical changing. Into it put outworn or dysfunctional attitudes and things that the dying one wishes to reprocess. Take the ashes and scatter them in a nearby field; visualize crops, flowers or other growing things rising from the enriched soil.)

21. Sea of Glass. Water is a great cleanser. Use this island as a place to cleanse the soul. (Visualize and bathe in the sea. Arise fresh and renewed in soul.)

22. Sea of Mist. Air is the medium of life. The soul-friend should explore this island gently, encouraging the dying one to feel the inspiration of air as new energy coming into the body, and the expiration of air as the waste energy passing away. Draw the analogy of human beings needing oxygen, derived from green vegetation, and the needs of trees and growing things to 'breathe' carbon dioxide, which human beings breathe out. What is waste air to one species is life to another. Note that a graduated form of guided-imagery may be necessary for this island. The dying one may experience the monster of this island as a predator who will snatch his or her breath away. Care should be taken not to create panic. On no account use this island with those who have respiratory difficulties. An alternative method might be to help the dying one experience inhaling as receiving the Divine Spirit and to experience exhaling as a prayerful gift.

23. Island of Recognition. On the very threshold of death, many realizations, last-minute doubts or concerns may arise. These may seem trivial to the soul-friend, but should be seen as unfinished business. If the concern can be assuaged by direct action, all care should be taken to do so. (Visualize this island. Cast the hazel-nut back to the thrower, resolving at the same time to leave all cares behind in this world.)

24. Island of the Rainbow Stream. All native cultures take care to leave food for the journey in the tombs of the departed. Use this island to explore the food you most desire that will strengthen you for the journey. If it is still possible to eat and drink normally, a simple feast may be enjoyed. The dying one can plan the food for the wake, to give pleasure and the communion of a shared meal with the bereaved. (Visualize this island and finding and eating the food you most desire.)

25. Pillar of the Silver Net. The process of passing through death can be explored at this point. Dying is a skill like any other and can only be practised through visualization. (Read this part of the *immram* to the dying one and together decide what scenario of passage is appropriate: it may be seen, for example, as passing through a wall, or a door in a wall, a hole in a tree, a garden gate etc.)

26. Island of the Shuttered Door. The prospect of what lies beyond death may be intriguing or frightening. Gently explore this island, but do not insist if the dying one does not feel prepared. (Visualize arriving at the island and open the door. Stress that there is no obligation to go through, but peer within or look through a little grating in the door. Discuss what is seen.)

27. Island of Women. One of the most painful separations is that of partners. Use this island to explore unassuaged desires, past or present lovers, and things that you most want to say. This island can also be explored by the remaining partner. A common problem among bereaved partners is not having had the opportunity to say what they really felt to the dying one. Allow both partners a private time to let down the barriers of reserve so that such communication is enabled.

28. Island of Berries. This island can explore the healing dreams of sleep and the approaching forgetfulness of life's troubles. It can also be a gentle way of 'healing' the body to death, the gradual laying down of responsibilities and worries.

29. Island of the Eagle. Explore this island to help the dying one create a spiritual body of health and vigour. (Enter the lake to be restored and emerge totally transformed in whatever form is desired.)

30. Island of Joy. Explore the joyful events of the dying one's life, which can be re-created here.

31. Island of Circled Fire. The fullness of blessedness waits on this island. Let the dying one enter this island and prepare a gathering of friends, living or dead. Here everyone meets harmoniously.

32. Island of Otters. This is the island on which to explore the necessity for forgiveness. Being unable to forgive forges links that connect the dying one to others. Such links can impede the process of death and cause great distress and anger. (Use the otters as ambassadors between the dying one and others.)

33. Island of the Falcon. As death approaches, the dying one will attune more closely to the promptings of the inner worlds. Imperceptible signals or tokens of death may come in dreams, giving licence to depart. This island can become a kind of beacon or watch-tower for such signals.

METHOD OF SOUL-LEADING

This method of soul-leading is recommended for people who have a diagnosed fatal condition, who may be in a hospice or are being cared for at home or in hospital. It can, of course, be done by any people who wish consciously to prepare for death as they reach the end of their years. The soul-friend should acquaint the dying one with the story of the *Voyage of Maelduin*, and the *immram* tradition, drawing parallels with other cultural and spiritual traditions related to death and the voyage over the sea.

The soul-friend must be both adaptable and sensitive to the needs of the dying one. Prime requirements are privacy and quietness for the sake of confidentiality and ease of practising the soul-leading. As a preliminary session, I suggest that the soul-friend encourages the dying one to discuss her or his needs, anxieties and concerns frankly; this will give the soul-friend a better idea of how to proceed. Let the dying one speak as much or little as is needed. The soul-friend may prompt by asking clarifying questions, but should listen as much as possible. Outline the nature of the soul-leading to the dying one and answer her or his questions. The soul-leading will help clarify, resolve and lay to rest certain life issues that now make their resurgence at the time of death.

For the next session, it is suggested that the soul-friend uses a graduated form of shamanic journey and guided-imagery work, describing a voyage and asking the dying one to imagine the scenes described. For those who are bed-ridden and have many long, empty or painful hours, an ongoing story is often a great help and distraction from the laborious business of dying. You will need to choose islands that tally with the concerns of the dying one. Consult the list of topics on pages 129 to 132.

For dying children, choose islands that reinforce

their sense of creative play. Encourage them to join in the story and participate; ask them to describe aloud the scenes they see and let them draw, model or paint them. This is also very therapeutic for adults who may not often have expressed themselves creatively since childhood. Much can be transmitted and understood by the artistic process that can never be conveyed in words.

There may be a tendency in the soul-friend to ignore the islands that have fearful or disturbing images on them and to stress the beautiful and harmonious ones. Let the dying one be allowed to handle the *immram* cards and pick out particular islands as ones to explore. You may also discover which cards the dying one feels uneasy about and explore the reasons why as sensitively as possible, bringing them into the guided-imagery *immram*. The dying one's own inner scenarios and spiritual beliefs should be incorporated within the journey and will arise naturally in the course of soul-leading. The soul-friend is merely facilitating the process and, if directed to change or modify the narration, should speedily do so.

It is advisable that the soul-friend be present at the moment of death and that this has been discussed with the dying one. There may be a particular island or islands to which the dying one wishes to be piloted at this time. A short ritual restatement of all good things enjoyed by the dying one may be made, the soul-friend calling each of these to be present to assist him or her: animals, gardens, friends, relatives, spiritual beings etc. Care should be taken to ensure that the ambiance of the death-room is harmonious: the dying one's favourite music may be played; flowers, images or favourite objects should be nearby. Relatives or friends who are too overcome with grief should be conducted outside so as not to disturb the process of dying, but they should not be excluded from being in the dying one's presence and should be given access at the moment of passing.

Old friends now deceased may welcome the dying one, as may spiritual beings into the realms beyond life. Island 25, the Pillar of the Silver Net, should be visited often in preparation for the moment of passing, visualizing the clear, calm sea that lies beyond the net.

It is possible that the family of the dying one has different ideas to those of him or her concerning preparation for death, and the religious and funeral arrangements. At all times, arrangements should be made to help the dying one make their own *immram* without fuss, and without fuelling any family drama. The soul-leading described here can be done by any person of any or no religious background, and is especially appropriate for someone who wishes to draw upon a neutral tradition. Memories of the dying one's religious up-bringing may well make an orthodox religious approach to death inappropriate or painful. The soul-friend should stress that the soul-leading is based upon a traditional teaching story common to spiritual traditions the world over. The actual soul-leading enables the deceased's soul to find its own way in peace.

DEPARTING THE SOUL-SHRINE CEREMONY

The actual moment of death can be marked by this adaptation of the Scots Gaelic ritual: it has been amended here to be used with people of all or any religious affiliation, but please adapt it to your own particular needs.

At the approach of death recite the soul-shrine prayer:

O Being of Brightness, Friend of Light,
  From the Blessed Realms of Grace,
Gently encircle me, sweetly enclosing me,
Guarding my soul-shrine from harm this
      day/night.

Keep me from anguish, keep me from danger,
Encircle my voyage over the seas.
A light will you lend me, to keep and
defend me,
O Beautiful Being, O Guardian this day/night.

Be a guiding star above me,
Illuminate each rock and tide,
Guide my ship across the waters,
To the waveless harbourside.

This can be recited by all present, or by the soul-friend alone while the others silently visualize the presence of strong spiritual helpers who will receive the departing soul. As the soul-shrine prayer is said, the soul-friend may anoint the dying one with oil to sain and strengthen him or her, signing the oil with a sacred gesture (sign of the Cross, a circled Celtic Cross, a star or whatever symbol seems appropriate) upon the forehead.

When the dying one breathes no more, the soul-friend may say:

Now is the soul set free,
Rising from the soul-shrine.
O Holy Eternal Ones from the Realms of Bliss,
Encircle the one we love in your own compassion.

The soul-friend and those present should visualize the departing soul as an ascending globe of coloured light. Now visualize a larger globe of golden light descending. The golden globe embraces and encloses the globe of the soul. The soul-friend or whoever wishes to, should remain in vigil over the soul-shrine for a decent time. The soul-shrine deserves respect, for it has been the vessel of the soul for many years.

It is very important, if this is taking place in a hospital, that hospital staff should not disturb the body for a full hour at least. Special permission may be obtained to hold a longer vigil but, in many cases, hospital routine insists on the removal of the body as soon as possible. Undertakers usually have a chapel of rest where the soul-shrine may be attended. If the death takes place at home, there will be greater ease to this ceremony. The soul-friend may also lead or attend the funeral and assist the bereaved family.

Please amend this ceremony or incorporate into it whichever elements have arisen from the soul-leading. It is important that the soul-friend should enable the process of death without dictating its order or method.

Whether you use *The Celtic Book of the Dead* for exploring your problems or preparing for a different mode of existence, I wish you a fruitful and exciting *immram*. May the Angels and Bright Ones guide you skilfully over the waters of the deep sea!

I would be interested in hearing from any readers who have conducted their own soul-leading. You can write to me at BCM HALLOWQUEST, London WC1N 3XX, England, enclosing a SAE or two international reply-paid coupons if you would like a reply.

Immram Chant

I do not know where I am bound.
I journey far across the foam.
I seek my soul, where is it found?
I watch the star to guide me home.

There is an island in the West
Under the sun, over the sea,
I travel far upon my quest.
I seek a guide to pilot me.

A branch of silver in my hand
With crystal bloom and golden fruit,
The mother tree grows on the strand;
It's there that I shall find my root.

There is an island in the sea,
Where waters flow and food gives life,
Where is no foe, where love is free.
I seek the place where is no strife.

I watch the star to guide me home,
I found my soul and spirit's rest,
I travelled far across the foam.
There is no ending to my quest.

Caitlín Matthews

ibliography

(All books are published in London unless otherwise stated.)

Ashe, Geoffrey. *Land to the West; St Brendan's Voyage to America*, Collins, 1962

Brown, Arthur L. 'Barinthus' in *Révue Celtique XXII*, pp. 339–344

Cross, T.P. & Slover, C.H. *Ancient Irish Tales*, Figgis, 1936

Cunliffe, Barry. *The Celtic World*, Bodley Head, 1979

Danaher, Kevin. *The Year in Ireland*, Mercier Press, 1972

Ellis, Peter Berresford. *The Celtic Empire*, Constable, 1990

Evans-Wentz, W.Y. *The Tibetan Book of the Dead*, Oxford University Press, 1960

Harner, Michael. *The Way of the Shaman*, Harper & Row, 1980

Kübler-Ross, Elisabeth. *Questions and Answers on Death & Dying*, Collier Macmillan, 1974

Levine, Stephen. *Healing into Life & Death*, Bath, Gateway Books, 1989

Lodö, Ven. Lama. *Bardo Teachings: the Way of Death & Rebirth*, Ithaca, Snow Lion, 1982

Loffler, Christa Maria. *The Voyage to the Otherworld Island in Early Irish Literature*, Salzburg, Institut für Anglistik und Amerikanistik, Universität Salzburg, 1983

Matthews, Caitlín. *Arthur and the Sovereignty of Britain*, Arkana, 1989

Matthews, Caitlín. *The Elements of Celtic Tradition*, Element, 1989

Matthews, Caitlín. *The Elements of the Goddess*, Element, 1989

Matthews, Caitlín. *Mabon and the Mysteries of Britain*, Arkana, 1987

Matthews, Caitlín. *Sophia, Goddess of Wisdom*, Mandala, 1990

Matthews, Caitlín and John. *The Arthurian Book of Days*, Sidgwick & Jackson, 1990

Matthews, Caitlín and John. *The Arthurian Tarot*, Aquarian, 1990

Matthews, Caitlín and John. *Hallowquest: Tarot Magic and the Arthurian Mysteries*, Aquarian, 1990

Matthews, Caitlín and John. *Ladies of the Lake*, Aquarian, 1992

Matthews, Caitlín and John. *The Western Way*, vol. 1, Arkana, 1985

Matthews, John. *The Celtic Shaman*, Element, 1991

Matthews, John. *Taliesin: the Bardic & Shamanic Mysteries in Britain and Ireland*, Aquarian, 1990

Meyer, Kuno and Nutt, Alfred. *The Voyage of Bran Son of Febal*, David Nutt, 1895

O'Meara, John J. *The Voyage of Saint Brendan: Journey to the Promised Land*, Dublin, Dolmen Press, 1978

Oskamp, H.P.A. *The Voyage of Mael Duin*, Groningen, 1970

Parry, John Jay. *The Vita Merlini*, University of Illinois, 1925

Patch, Howard Rollin. *The Other World*, Cambridge, Mass., Harvard University Press, 1950

Picard, J-M, and de Pontfarcy, Y. *Saint Patrick's Purgatory*, Dublin, Four Courts Press, 1985

Rees, Alwyn and Brinley. *Celtic Heritage*, Thames & Hudson, 1988

Severin, Tim. *The Brendan Voyage*, Arena, 1978

Sherr, Lorraine (ed.). *Death, Dying & Bereavement*, Oxford, Blackwell Scientific Publications, 1989.

Spaan, David Bruce, 'The Otherworld in Early Irish Literature', Doctoral dissertation, University of Michigan, 1969

Stevens, Jose & Lena. *Secrets of Shamanism*, Avon Books, 1988

Stewart, R.J. *Advanced Magical Arts*, Element, 1988

Stewart, R.J. *The Underworld Initiation*, Aquarian, 1989

Wood-Martin, W.G. *Traces of the Elder Faiths of Ireland*, Longmans, Green & Co., 1902

RESOURCES

A journey tape of singing and drumming can be obtained from Caitlín Matthews at BCM HALLOWQUEST, London WC1N 3XX. Please send SAE for details (within UK) or two international reply-paid coupons if writing from outside the UK. You will be sent full details of this and other tapes relating to working the *immram* as shamanic journey. Please note that tuitional tapes are only available in the English language. The author is available to give workshops on the *immram* and other subjects.